DO YOU KNOW WHAT YOU'RE DOING, GOD?

• • • • • •

Unveiling a Spirituality for the Twenty-First Century

• • • • • •

Louis DeThomasis, FSC

i.e.

in extenso

DO YOU KNOW WHAT YOU'RE DOING, GOD?
Unveiling a Spirituality for the Twenty-First Century
by Louis DeThomasis, FSC

Edited by Michael Coyne
Cover and text design and typesetting by Patricia A. Lynch, Harvest Graphics

Cover photo "The Veiled Christ" © Pietro Scolorato.

Published by In Extenso Press
Distributed exclusively by ACTA Publications, 4848 N. Clark Street,
Chicago, IL 60640, (800) 397-2282, www.actapublications.com

Scripture quotations from the *New Revised Standard Version Bible*, copyright
© 1989 by the Division of Christian Education of the National Council of the Churches of Christ in the USA. Used by permission.

Scripture quotations from *The Message: Catholic/Ecumenical Edition*, copyright ©
2013 by Eugene H. Petersen. All rights reserved. Licensed with permission of Nav-
Press. Represented by Tyndale House Publishers Inc. Carol Stream, Illinois 60188.

Library of Congress Catalog Number: 2017950193
Hardcover ISBN: 978-0-87946-978-8
Paperback ISBN: 978-0-87946-979-5
Printed in the United States of America by Total Printing Systems
Year 30 29 28 27 26 25 24 23 22 21 20 19 18
Printing 15 14 13 12 11 10 9 8 7 6 5 4 3 2

♻ Text printed on 30% post-consumer recycled paper

CONTENTS

INTRODUCTION

God Will Answer Us

· · · · · ·

*We thought that after the [Vatican II] Council there would be
a day of sunshine for the history of the Church, and instead we
found storms.*

POPE PAUL VI

· · · · · ·

A nd storms there still are! We faithful who are out in today's freewheeling information age know that the religious world has not escaped the storms that have buffeted politics, society, and culture. The blustery squalls coming from global diversity, rapid changes in the political landscape, terrorism, and brutal conflicts on six continents have few parallels in history—ancient or modern. Those strong gusts swirling all around the globe rattle any hopes of serenity and tranquility in our lives. Is it possible for any of us not to feel those very storms jolting us to our spiritual cores? In fact, for the faithful Catholic, there is no need to even step outside our own church doors to be blasted by that tempest. The windstorms of controversy and contretemps are just as present within our parish church and also, maybe even especially, within the frescoed walls of the Vatican itself. Indeed, opening the Catholic Church's stained glass windows at Vatican II let in a lot more than bright sunshine and fresh air.

Let me be direct from the outset and step out into the storms of ecclesial wrangling, bickering, and full-fledged battles. Of course, many readers—or should I say potential readers—may disapprove, or at least be curious about, the title that I chose for a book about spirituality: *Do You Really Know What*

You Are Doing, God? Unveiling a Spirituality for the Twenty-First Century. At first some may think it just doesn't make any sense to question God. How much more perplexing, then, is it for me to assert that questioning is not just permissible, but that it is an essential element of any mature spirituality? Does that sound over the top? Is that an arrogant, sacrilegious, or at the very least impertinent question that should rightfully bring the wrath of God raining down upon me? Isn't it also a baffling question, since we believe the omnipotent Creator and Savior and Spirit of the World to be all knowing? And finally, realizing that question places me in the eye of the storm of today's church controversy, isn't it heretical for me to even entertain such a question?

I don't think so. In fact, I wrote this book because I believe it is my obligation as a vowed religious, a lifelong educator, and a faithful Catholic to ask that very prying question and many more like it. I do not claim to present on these pages an academic theological presentation. Many magnificent works from astute professional theologians address these confusing times in the church from a more academic perspective. Their contributions are incredibly valuable—despite the fact that some of our church leaders dismiss many of their thoughts and insights as unorthodox or even outright heresy. While I am no theologian, I am definitely an expert about my personal faith. That is, I am a faith-filled, doubt-filled, and question-filled believer in the Catholic Church as the People of God and—as best I am able—a follower of Jesus Christ. I present this book as an individual Christian, specifically a Catholic believer on a life-long journey exploring how I, a sinner, can better follow Jesus Christ in today's world and under a church hierarchy whose actions often confuse and confound me.

I am frustrated with the tensions and attacks by both the ideologically rigid Catholic conservatives and the similarly uncompromising Catholic liberals. I don't even like the placaters who claim the middle of the road. This state of affairs in the Catholic Church is as much the fault of church insiders as outsiders;

• • • • • •

Questioning is not just permissible, but it is an essential element of any mature spirituality.

• • • • • •

priests as well as laypeople; bishops as well as cardinals and popes. Certainly, not everyone in each of those categories is a perpetrator of divisiveness; but, I am firmly convinced that even those who remain silent are just as much at fault because they are not publicly out front, condemning the destructive antagonism that seems to overwhelm our institution. This is not the way Christians should be seeking solutions to the many legitimate differences among us. Where are the realists and innovators in the church who are ready and willing to use Christian common sense to create the future of "your kingdom come… on earth as it is in heaven," rather than endlessly indulging in nostalgia for a perfect church of the past that all educated Catholics understand never really existed?

The general state of Catholic spirituality has failed to ameliorate this unfortunate state of affairs. It's just not working. Woefully lacking is a necessary, generous dose of Christian common sense. Enough already of traditional and nostalgic spirituality that was considered by some to be effective in the past. Enough of the forced rationalizations within dogmatic teachings that pretend the Catholic Church can never change its doctrines. In case we haven't observed, the world is not just changing—it has already changed. The church, as well, is not just changing—it has already changed. People have changed; politics have changed; culture has changed. What makes anyone think it is possible that the church has not changed?

I will argue throughout this book that the core truth of God's love for creation and the loving care of the divine Holy Trinity for that creation has not changed. It can never change. But that is about all that has not changed—and will never change. The rest is up for grabs, whether the church's leaders and bureaucrats like it or not.

For the Catholic Church to remain relevant today, it is important that we are free, and even encouraged, to talk about Christian truths in ways that people can understand them, and to develop a spirituality that embraces change instead of denying and resisting it. The Catholic Church must offer people—especially our young people—a spirituality that proclaims the Gospel message of love for all without condemnatory bias toward anyone. Anything less is not Christian, and therefore not Catholic.

You are not alone if you say this kind of unbiased spirituality is not humanly possible. I would have to agree. But neither is it a human impossibility to transform our spirituality into one that is inclusive, open, and loving to all. That is Christian common sense, if we embrace the spirit of Jesus' Gospel by following him in how he loved and served unconditionally. As Saint Paul put it: "We are fools for the sake of Christ, but you are wise in Christ. We are weak, but you are strong. You are held in honor, but we in disrepute." (1 Corinthians 4:10) While loving and serving unconditionally may appear to be folly, it happens to be the unwavering demand of the Gospel. Of course such love and service seem to be humanly impossible, but isn't that what Christianity is all about?

God created a world that is good—in fact, Scripture tells us it's very good. Neither you, nor I, nor the Catholic Church created our very good world, whose imprint reflects the image and likeness of God. It's now the Christian's mission to nurture, through love and service, a continuation of that ongoing creation of our very good world. This article of faith can be appreciated to the degree that we see a reflection of the diversity of Three Divine Persons reflected in the abundance of diversity in people, ideas, and beliefs surrounding us. Difference, variety, mixture, discrepancy, and ambiguity is *in*, *through*, and *with* God's Creation. There isn't just one way to love and serve each person on Earth. That's just plain common sense. So how can a true Christian spirituality be a rigid construct that does not embrace diversity? It must encompass the same diversity that the Trinity's reality reflects: the One God in Three Divine Persons. The "one" God apparently needed that diversity to express "oneness"— what a mystery that is! Divine ambiguity may look like human folly, but we Christians call it revelation.

As I warned above, this book is not an academic theological treatise; yet, I hope to assimilate the work of many fine theologians in an understandable manner for serious and thoughtful Christians who are not satisfied with the conventional spirituality we are offered by the Catholic Church today. I invite the reader not to approach this book as a dogmatic presentation, even though I state my convictions quite forthrightly. One of my friends scolded me once after I told her that I was being forthright with her, saying, "Louis, you're forthright all right—you are right only about 25% of the time." So, I leave it to my reader to judge which "fourth" of this book is correct.

Please read this book with pen in hand. Question it; argue with it; explore with it; then ask God your own questions. Be questioning, and yet have faith. God will answer you. That's spirituality for sure. You can be certain of that because the validity of the examined Christian life sustains our certitude that Jesus lives in our hearts forever.

Louis DeThomasis, FSC, Ph.D.
Rome, Italy
Pentecost Sunday, 2017

CHAPTER 1

Better Late Than Never

• • • • • •

If one takes seriously the Incarnation—that is, that God made himself part of history—it's impossible to think of doctrine as fixed code that came down from heaven.

Antonio Spadaro, SJ

• • • • • •

We Christians have our own important questions to ask if we desire to deepen our spiritual lives through our personal faith commitment to Jesus. There are, of course, equally compelling questions to ask if we desire to deepen our fidelity to the Catholic Church. And if we want to truly understand the relationship between our own faith and the teachings of the institutional church, there are even more questions to explore.

While we should all be asking questions, many of us today are afraid we will experience blowback from the church if we ask our most personal and perplexing questions. It seems counter-intuitive to find that kind of tension in the church community, but the piercing questions of which I speak are not welcomed by many in the hierarchy. Answers that the Catholic Church does provide through its teachings often indicate that it doesn't seem to understand people's current needs and concerns. Just as conventional solutions are failing us in the political arena today, traditional answers are just not working for all the faithful in the church. Be aware, it is not the truth of the Christian Gospel and God's revelations that are not working; rather, it's the "how's" and "what's" of many official hierarchal pronouncements that are irrelevant or unresponsive to many of the faithful's lived experiences, the questions and legitimate doubts we bear.

This point is amply demonstrated in the results of two national studies from the *Center for Applied Research in the Apostolate at Georgetown University* [CARA]. In an interview conducted by Matt Hadro of the *Catholic News Agency* (December 18, 2016), Mark Gray, a senior research associate at CARA said of their findings about young Catholics:

> *It's almost a crisis in faith.... In the whole concept of faith, this is a generation that is struggling with faith in ways that we haven't seen in previous generations.*

These studies show quite clearly that this crisis has occurred in part because the hierarchy's teachings are not compatible with things demonstrated by basic science to be unequivocally true. Most alarming are findings revealed in Gray's interview about the age at which the faithful begin to fall away: "The interviews with youth and young adults who had left the Catholic faith revealed that the typical age for this decision to leave was made at 13.... Nearly two-thirds of those surveyed, 63 percent, said they stopped being Catholic between the ages of 10 and 17. Another 23 percent say they left the faith before the age of 10." Of those who had left the faith, "only 13 percent said they were ever likely to return to the Catholic Church...and absent any big changes in their life they are probably not coming back."

If the institutional church does not read the signs of the times now, and transform its spirituality now, there may be no viable future for a Catholic Church that is inclusive and is for all people across the globe. It will be, instead, just what some in the Vatican and elsewhere (but not our current pope, Francis) are calling for: a church that is smaller but ostensibly more "faithful." Of course, what these church hierarchs mean by "faithful" is that the rest of us accept what they themselves proclaim to be the acceptable practice of Catholic faith.

It is not just the young, but even the older faithful who have questions about, and the desire to examine, traditional Catholic teachings. For example, we Catholics have always believed that Jesus is truly God, yet he is also truly human, and not just God pretending to be human. Even in the midst of global tensions and frightful acts of terrorism today, most of us continue to believe that core truth. But some of us wonder how or why an all-knowing God took on a human nature and came into this sinful world. No one in the history of the world has been able to offer a complete understanding of that singular act, of the divine becoming human. Not even the magisterium of the Catholic Church can offer a definitive explanation of how the Incarnation is possible. It only teaches that it is true. And we who have faith believe it, even if we don't understand it.

But we now know and cannot dismiss the fact that most people in Jesus' time neither understood nor believed his claim that he was God. These are the very people who heard, saw, and lived with him during his earthly life. Not only did they not believe; they condemned him to death. Yes, the very people who directly experienced him, his teachings, his love, and his many miracles wanted him dead. How, as a human being to whom God has given the gift of intellect, can I not ask, "Did you really know what you were doing to your son, God?"

If we believe that Jesuit Father Antonio Spadaro (the editor of *Civiltà Cattolica*) showed keen insight in the epigraph to this chapter, then surely we can acknowledge that there is no "fixed code," nor any ironclad heavenly dissertation explaining the Mystery of Faith. Isn't that why we call it a mystery? We must admit we will never fully understand the mystery of the Divine Trinity; or the rationality of Jesus dying so that we may live; or a full explanation for God's omnipotence and infinite love; or reasons why people are as they are—astounding, loving, miraculous, awesome, and yet, at times, sinful, hurtful, judgmental, and inconsiderate! Never mind the implications of that for the Church's catechesis; try explaining that to yourself without asking God any questions.

As Christians we believe that Jesus, the only begotten Son of God, is the

Savior of the world and that he lived, died, and rose from the dead because he loves us, sinful though we may be. That bit of truth takes a large chunk of faith and can never be fully captured—or co-opted—by institutionalized religion with all its dogmas, doctrines and dictums. Those mysteries are not picture puzzles that can be assembled into a total picture of the reality of God's creation. It is truly a mystery, and while puzzles can be solved, mysteries can never be unraveled. At best we may embrace and live with a spirituality encapsulated in personal faith that finds its life in the seeking of understanding. But, such a spirituality cannot be realized without exploring—and questioning—that which is not completely knowable in human terms. If one's faith does not have more "I don't know" than "Here's the answer" then it is not faith. It is superstition or folklore.

If one's faith does not have more "I don't know" than "Here's the answer" then it is not faith.

With the teachings of Jesus' church and its Tradition over the years we are in a continual process of becoming Christians—never to be fully consummated in this life—who follow Jesus in love and service, even with our questions and doubts. As devout Christians we should be on a never ending journey of becoming, seeking, and discovering Jesus Christ. As our spirituality matures, we find a growing confidence to explore the very doubts and questions that we might have once feared were signs of weak faith.

As we pray and question God for understanding, we may often find ourselves surprised that instead of discovering all the answers, we reveal more and better questions to ask, and unearth more doubts to contend with. As the popular adage instructs us, there is a higher truth in questions that can't be answered than in answers that can't be questioned. Questions, not answers, can simultaneously deepen and strengthen our fidelity to our faith in the church as the People of God.

Institutional religions, through their doctrines, ideologies, and even the magisterium of the Catholic Church, honestly attempt to reveal religious truths. Yet those efforts necessarily obscure the totality of those divine mysteries. Mystical truths are beyond human comprehension. However those religious truths are expressed in human language, that expression can, at best, only assist us in our own embrace of those hidden mysteries of faith.

Rigid doctrinal attempts to explain complex religious concepts in simple terms may actually hinder many in their quest for an informed faith—especially the young. When formalized religion attempts to proclaim its faith, it seems designed often more to provide a veil obscuring the entire truth than a lens helping us to discern ever deeper truths. It is through our own spirituality that we must begin to lift that veil in order to better see—in the very act of lifting—the truth lying beneath, within, and beyond. The Catholic Church and its teachings, for example, attempt to reveal a divine reality that cannot be contained—God's unconditional and limitless love for us and all of creation. Paradoxical as it may seem, we Catholics need a spirituality that will nurture questioning and doubting within the communion of the universal church.

Perhaps this image of a veil may be better understood by tapping into our imaginations with the kind of insights that great works of art can awaken in us. Specifically, I am in awe of Giuseppe Sanmartino's (1720-1793) sculpture that sits in the Sansevero Chapel (*Capella Sansevero de' Sangri*) in Naples, Italy. Though this masterpiece, *The Veiled Christ*, is not as famous as Michelangelo's *Pietà* or his *David*, it is as magnificent, astonishing, and perhaps—because of its relative obscurity—even more wondrous.

When beholding *The Veiled Christ*, it is impossible not to be mesmerized by the illusion of the sculpted veil that covers Jesus' reposed body. This marble veil, implausibly and remarkably, appears to be translucent. The viewer can actually see the image of Jesus' body, as if through this sculpted marble veil. So translucent in appearance is the veil that our vision informs us that the veil could not possibly have been sculpted from marble. For centuries, many conjectured that the veil was indeed a fake, processed to look like marble, counterfeit, since it was believed no sculptor could execute such an extraordinary illusion. Many hypothesized that an actual veil was placed over Sanmartino's sculpted Christ and some chemical machinations utilized to create the illusion that the shroud was marble. Modern scientific analysis, however, confirms that the veil in this masterpiece is truly and totally sculptured of marble. It's truly amazing.

We Christians have faith in Jesus Christ, who we believe is the only Son of God in a unique and special way that we, who are also children of God, do not share. We are in joyful communion within the church as the People of God *as we lift together* the veil of faith, of our doctrine of the Trinity, to comprehend more completely the nature of our loving God. We proclaim our faith in the God of Jesus, in spite of the fact that we have no certifiable proof that God is as Jesus described him. Our Jesus is now a veiled Christ, and our God has always been a veiled Holy Trinity. Throughout our lives as Christians, it is our own spirituality that empowers us to lift the veil covering divine mystery, little by little, throughout our faith journey in this mortal life. But we also believe that until we meet our Lord in his loving embrace, until we are born into eternal life, that veil can never be fully lifted.

Jesus is a puzzle that humans can never put together completely. He is the mystery that we embrace in a relationship with God through the grace of faith. This brings us together, in communion, with all his followers in a loving acceptance of the abundant diversity of God's creation.

Why, then, can we not have a spirituality in today's world that flourishes and grows with dialogue, questions, and doubts, even within the institutional church itself? Or perhaps, the better question is, "Can we any longer have a meaningful Christian spirituality without an abiding faith that still has questions or doubts?" Should questioning make us feel guilty, or cause us to doubt our faith? No. In today's world, our skepticism should be a sign of true faith.

It's about time in our modern, globalized world, that the Catholic Church and its teaching authorities, along with all religions and all people of good will, stop acting as if a scant few of us have a monopoly on truth, stop the pretense that anyone can lay claim to a singular understanding of God that alone is real. It's about time, in this shrinking globe of ours, that we accept diverse ways of loving, discerning, and believing. Such acceptance would not weaken our faith as a Church; it would rather nourish and expand our insights into an all-loving God.

Do we forget that even the disciples—who lived, ate, and drank with him and witnessed his miracles first-hand—doubted Jesus many times? Peter— *"the rock I will build my church on"*—denied Jesus three times in his hour of passion. Thomas refused to believe in the resurrected Jesus until he had placed his hands in Jesus' wounds. Should we now, two thousand years later, be troubled because we have doubts and questions for the successors to those same doubting disciples? Eugene H. Peterson captures this very familiar scriptural moment in his modern translation, *The Message*:

> *Thomas said, "My Master! My God!" Jesus said, "So, you believe because you've seen with your own eyes. Even better blessings are in store for those who believe without seeing." Jesus provided far more God-revealing signs than are written down in this book. These are written down so you will believe that Jesus is the Messiah, the Son of God, and in the act of believing, have real and eternal life in the way he personally revealed it.*

> John 20: 28-32

The Catholic Church, through its doctrines, tries to explain the beliefs at the core of our shared Christian faith. These explanations, however, turn out to be much like the illusion of the veil in Sanmartino's sculpture of *The Veiled Christ*. While they are not fabrications or intentional machinations of the truth, they do shroud the real mystery of our God and Savior, which is neither scientifically verifiable nor easily captured in words.

The very means intended to help us understand Christianity act instead as a veil—not of marble—but of words, creeds, and dogmas. These are the veils covering Jesus today. We come to know *about our God* when we actively seek out the teachings of our church and participate in communal rituals, sacraments, and prayers. But, we can only come *to our God* when we personally experience the divine life in our own spiritual lives.

This book attempts to help readers lift the veil cloaking the essence of our Christian faith and rediscover its robust spirituality. It is my very personal and common sense reflection on the world that I have experienced and cherished my entire life, and on the Roman Catholic Church that I have loved and served my entire ministry.

Beware! It will not be a comfortable ride—no safe and secure spiritual journey replete with pat answers. Together let's peel back that veil so that we may more clearly encounter in new ways the Jesus of the Scriptures in this confounding and convoluted world of ours. Let's exercise the spiritual maturity to ask: "Do you really know what you are doing, God?"

CHAPTER 2

From Magic to Faith…
But Faith in What?

· · · · · ·

"I want to do it properly," were the first words of which Harry was
fully conscious of speaking. "Not by magic. Have you got a spade?"
And shortly afterward he had set to work, alone, digging the grave
in the place that Bill had shown him at the end of the garden,
between bushes. He dug with a kind of fury, relishing the manual
work, glorying in the non-magic of it, for every drop of his sweat
and every blister felt like a gift to the elf who had saved their lives.

J.K. ROWLING
HARRY POTTER AND THE DEATHLY HALLOWS

· · · · · ·

For much of history, people looked upon the forces of nature as perplexing and capricious. Shamans typically claimed ownership of secret remedies, or ritualistic prayers to the deities to influence nature's mysterious ways, or the sacrifice of animals—and sometimes even humans—to appease the mercurial gods. Diseases were attributed to transgressions against the spirits, climatic disruptions were considered signs of the gods' displeasure, and evil spirits needed to be inveigled with all manner of hocus-pocus by an elite and privileged class.

Tom Carney, in a *National Catholic Reporter* article (September 20, 2016) titled "Our intelligence is a gift from a generous creator," captures the reality of the religious predisposition to magic that can so easily subsume spiritual faith when he writes:

I often hear prayers in church or elsewhere that appeal to this magician God. We ask God to do things God may expect us to do ourselves—like reducing poverty, putting an end to war, and taking care of the environment. Most bad things happen, ultimately, because we allow them.

For most of human history, we have understood that faith is in reality the prevailing force that propels peoples' lives in this world. Yes, faith. But faith in what? The religious impulse was what I would term more an "archetype" of faith than faith itself, usually manifested somehow through the reputed power of convoluted mystical forms. It was faith suspended like a fly in amber in practices and rituals controlled by entitled religious authorities. Followers sought a means to negotiate, through those intermediaries, with the inscrutable ways of nature and the divine. Some form of magic was deemed necessary for the simple reason that the natural order was so poorly understood until very recently in human history. This thought is perhaps nowhere more succinctly expressed than by George Coyne, SJ, retired director of the Vatican Observatory, who said: "My faith is rational, though not provable by scientific means. It means leaving behind "God the Magician."

Shades of the magical mystique still have an insidious but obscure—might we say veiled?—presence deep within the credos of modern religious institutions. Even in this third millennium, so dominated by science and technology, vestiges of mystical powers over the unexplained remain; such forces at least still abound in faith communities. On the opposite end of the spectrum, today's staunchest atheists—perhaps unconsciously but certainly paradoxically—apotheosize science itself, acting as if they are today's high priests, with a magical prowess in solving what they consider to be the problems worth solving. Might the Christian churches fuel such tendencies with our orthodox rituals and moral dictums that leave so little room for questioning?

It is our responsibility as thinking Christians to lift the veil covering Jesus when his message and image are blurred with spellbinding words or dictums from any individual or institution—profane, secular, or clericalist. It was Saint Augustine who advised us Christians that, "Believers are also thinkers; in believing they think, and in thinking they also believe.... If faith does not think, it is nothing."

Integrity requires the faithful to carefully consider how we Christians are incorporating our beliefs with modern secular advances in science, medicine, anthropology, and psychology. We must be especially attentive in articulating moral principles regarding such wide-ranging topics as the role of women; the role of sexuality in a variety of intimate relationships; the sensitivity to cultural diversity on today's shrinking globe; and even the investments we make and the actions we take to foster a love and respect for the environment and the integrity of creation—or fail to take.

We must think and judge for ourselves and inform our consciences with the teachings of the institutional church. We must judge in fairness whether the institutional church is articulating sound principles consistent with our modern understanding of the world. We must consider whether some church leader or institution inappropriately demands allegiance to nostalgic propositions that have been long disproved, or are laced with claims of infallibility that cannot be properly claimed. And we must ultimately accept our responsibility to form our own conscience, and to judge the way we do that with the same rigor we apply to our religious leaders and institutions.

A fully "informed" conscience requires thinking Christians to listen thoughtfully to the teachings of the institutional church, most of which are not proclaimed *"ex cathedra"* (an exceedingly rare event), but we can never be required to suspend our intellect or common sense in the process. We cannot be expected to check our brains at the church door, like so many unbefitting hats. We do well to heed the warning of Jose Ortega y Gasset (1883-1955), the highly regarded Spanish philosopher, when he said:

Better beware of notions like genius and inspiration; they are a sort of magic wand and should be used sparingly by anybody who wants to see things clearly.

It may be helpful to reflect on the Harry Potter epigraph that opens this chapter. Even in his awesome magical world with his mastery of the occult, Harry was found, "relishing the manual work, glorying in the non-magic of it, for every drop of his sweat and every blister felt like a gift…." Indeed, scientific and technological advances should give us all cause to place less emphasis on enchantment and more on enlightenment. A modern Christian should never be complacent, content with pietistic explanations of sanctified authority, whether it is veiled or whether it is wizard-like. Much as Harry Potter did, we accept our journey in Christian faith as a job of hard work with all the "sweat and blisters" it implies: asking the difficult questions; struggling with our doubts; stumbling over the many obstacles that appear daily without warning. This is how twenty-first century Christians seek a relationship with our loving Creator.

The Catholic Church has overtly acknowledged that traditional ways require transformation in today's world. In 2010, Pope Benedict XVI inaugurated the establishment of *The Pontifical Council for Promoting New Evangelization.* No matter what spin combatting institutional church players try to place on this development, the blatant fact is that Pope Benedict XVI—a respected traditional pontiff and theologian—saw the need for new ways of evangelizing for one obvious reason: The old one isn't working too well. Even after this admission by a conservative pope, and despite the pastoral ways of his successor, there are still deeply embedded institutional forces in the Vatican—and elsewhere—who fight change.

Unless we the faithful ask difficult and uncomfortable questions, and the church nurtures a new, open, and engaging spirituality, people both inside and outside the church will be confused. The institutional conflicts among the hierarchy are no longer secret. They are out in the open. For instance, on September 19, 2016, Cardinals Burke, Caffarra, Brandmuller, and Meisner made public five *dubia* (Latin for doubts) sent to Pope Francis demanding clarification on the document, *Amoris Laetitia*. Then, Cardinals Burke and Brandmuller indicated that if the pope does not respond to their *dubia* they will initiate some type of "formal correction" to him. (I guess the cultural war inside the institutional church has begun! And it has been started by the very traditionalist Cardinals who always objected if any of the rest of us faithful ever questioned what the pope said. Very interesting, isn't it?)

• • • • • •

If the hierarchy does not nurture a new evangelization with a spirituality for today's world, then we will continue to see true disenchantment.

• • • • • •

We laypeople, clerics, and vowed religious, who make up the great bulk of the people of God, can no longer rely on simple answers in a world that is increasingly complex. The traditionalists among the hierarchy are fighting their culture wars because they fear the faithful will be confused if they don't give them all the answers—packaged, approved, and requiring no further inspection. To the contrary, it is the traditionalists who are confusing us. If the hierarchy does not nurture a new evangelization with a spirituality for today's world, then we will continue to see true disenchantment—especially among our young people—as we reclaim our brains at the door and we shuffle out of church, searching for other institutions and other, secular, leaders to help us understand our modern human predicament.

Faithful Christians today certainly believe that God is all-knowing and infinite. But we also know that we humans are finite beings and can never have all the answers. So how on earth can we not have questions, doubts, and an incomplete understanding of a God who is totally "other" and therefore incomprehensible to finite minds? To think that anyone has complete knowledge about God, or that institutional church teachings have fully captured the mystery of God, is an illusion that taints our beautiful and life-affirming religion with distracting magical qualities. Rationality must be taken into account in the new evangelization if it is to make sense in today's world.

J.K. Rowling opined in one interview, "We do not need magic to transform our world. We carry all of the power we need inside ourselves already." That power is the grace of Christian faith, churning inside those who are willing to sweat and blister with the hard work of believing, serving, and acting upon Jesus' message to love all, despite the pervasive and inexplicable evil we find in the world we live in. The person who does not then ask, "Do you really know what you are doing, God?" is confusing spirituality with a magical certitude. That person fails to explore the richest questions hidden deep in the solitude of our soul's journey of faith.

A spirituality responsive to today's increasingly democratic and free-thinking world deepens our faith and blesses us with the confidence to share with God all our concerns, doubts, and questions. Oh yes, we have all heard orthodox proclamations that tell us God gave us free will and therefore does not cause evil in the world, but merely permits evil to exist. And that is supposed to make us feel better? Well, that explanation doesn't do the job for me!

More and more people—the young, the middle-aged, and the old—in our modern world are questioning the validity of the orthodox rationale that evil is not God's fault. It is not because we are less spiritual today but rather because we are eager and committed to live with an authentic spirituality that—despite our incomplete understanding—trusts in a divine Creator who loves and cares for all of creation. The growing lack of confidence in organized religions' easy answers emanates from a faith in a loving and merciful God that is not imbued with past rigid doctrines or magical forces. Our faith comes alive in today's world because the faithful respond to God's love with our actions, with our *sweat* and with our *blisters*.

So how can it be that an all-loving merciful and holy God does not cause, but supposedly only permits evil, in creation: unspeakable poverty, sickness, child abuse, death, starvation, terrorism justified in God's name, church scandals, and a never-ending list of horrors and injustices? It is up to the faithful Christian to have the courage and the loving relationship with God to ask the question, "Do you really know what you are doing, God?"

Today's ideological Christians are afraid to ask that question. They need a big dose of real, living faith. It is like two people who love each other: They trust enough to ask about things they don't understand about each other. That doesn't mean they don't love; rather it is proof of an abundance of love in their relationship. How much more, then, should we trust our God enough to ask questions about things we do not understand? Superstitious and unquestioning belief in God actually signifies distrust in God. It suggests that we may be trying to fool ourselves into believing that we possess magical powers that let us fully understand the omnipotent creator.

• • • • • •

The faith-filled Christian is willing to love and act on Christian love in this world even though there are no complete answers in life.

• • • • • •

The faith-filled Christian is willing to love and act on Christian love in this world even though there are no complete answers in life. We Christians who encounter Jesus in the Scriptures know Jesus did not come into this world as some magical security blanket to take away our responsibility to act with love for all—not just the few or even the many. That simply is not the Christian message. In my recent book, *All Things to All People: A Catholic Church for the Twenty-First Century*, I explore at length how faith-filled Christians must stop just "being Christians" by accepting institutional beliefs and "do Christianity" by following Jesus' Gospel of love for all. In that book I quote from Eugene Peterson's contemporary translation of the Bible, *The Message*:

> *Even though I am free of the demands and expectations of everyone, I have voluntarily become a servant to any and all in order to reach a wide range of people: religious, nonreligious, meticulous moralists, loose-living immoralists, the defeated, the demoralized—whoever. I didn't take on*

their way of life. I kept my bearings in Christ—but I entered their world and tried to experience things from their point of view. I've become just about every sort of servant there is in my attempts to lead those I meet into a God-saved life. I did all this because of the Message. I didn't just want to talk about it; I wanted to be in on it!

1 Corinthians 9:19-25

Jesus brought us salvation through love, yet there remains suffering; with mercy, yet there are still hardships; with caring, yet there is always brokenness; with faith, yet there is doubt and confusion. He called the people of his time to be holy people of action by serving others. He chastised the hypocrites, whether they were secular or religious leaders. It takes courage to live a life as a follower of Jesus when we know we lack pat answers to the biggest questions.

But that's Christian faith. That's Christian spirituality for today's world.

CHAPTER 3

Not "Born-Again Christians"...
But "Christianity Born Again"

· · · · · ·

Anyone who wishes to engage in the radical transformation of what exists will find tradition to be an indispensable source of content, inspiration, and caution. The proper attitude toward tradition is neither preservation nor rejection but to rethink the whole tradition with the help of present knowledge.

GABRIEL MORAN

· · · · · ·

Tensions, even disputes, persist among various Christian denominations in spite of significant progress in interreligious dialogue. Especially within the Catholic Church, differences abound. No one is immune: the pope, cardinals, bishops, deacons, vowed religious, and laity. Hot-button topics bring out destructive dynamics that bear no semblance to Christian charity: communion for divorced Catholics; same-sex marriage; LGBT church employees being fired; women's ordination; abortion and even birth control. The list goes on.

It would be disingenuous to deny that a veil obscures our vision of Christianity and Jesus' desire that we may all be one—with love for all. But the rancor so common among religious people today is inexplicable in the light of our shared biblical values. Many people ask themselves, "God, why do you permit such viciousness among different religions and even among faithful Christians themselves, much less among Roman Catholics? Do you realize the negative consequences for your church and the faithful?" Most of us fear to express such thoughts freely lest others judge us as unfaithful or sinful for asking such impertinent questions. Then the warring labels start flying: hypocrite, heretic, unfaithful, disordered, intrinsically evil, apostate.

We faithful followers of Jesus must act with love, care, and respect for others, even those with whom we disagree. It is when religion becomes *ideology* instead of *spirituality* that culture wars are fought. The ideologues' ammunition is labels: conservative vs. liberal, orthodox vs. heterodox, holy vs. worldly. But behind each of those labels are people who are Christians— whether we like it or not; whether we are like them or not; whether we agree with them or not; whether we are a cardinal or a lay person; whether we are a learned theologian or a simple carpenter.

It is important for us to remind ourselves of important clarifying distinctions between religion, faith, and spirituality. Those words are often used interchangeably in ordinary speech. Without elaborating on the many academic, theological, and philosophical nuances in these terms, however, I can surely state some simple but important distinguishing attributes of each.

A *religion* is usually understood to be a community of believers with a fixed set of beliefs, doctrines, and practices concerning the relationship between divinity and humanity. They are usually organized within well-defined institutional structures and join one another in a regular practice of ritualistic celebrations.

Faith is a universal phenomenon that may be experienced by people whether they are practicing a particular religion or not. To live in the world of faith, we must embrace a natural, universal form of belief in something: the discipline of science, the healing power of medicine, or the primal importance of our personal interactions with others. Even atheists may embrace some basic faith. It is simply believing in phenomena that cannot be totally proven by our senses but are nonetheless important to our world view.

In this book, I will explore, very specifically, Catholic *spirituality*. Spirituality, though somewhat distinct from and more than a set of doctrines or rituals, is inextricably related to both our faith and our practice of religion. When we accept the theses of any religion, when we accept as true its stated beliefs, those beliefs should activate a spirituality in our lives, an intimate response to our religion that places us on a personal journey to meet in relationship to God.

Spirituality is not necessarily following a particular type of liturgy or religious devotion; it is how we find meaning in our lives; how we live our lives in accord with our God; how we relate to people and ideas. For the Catholic faithful, it also includes our acceptance and grace-filled embrace of the sacraments. For us Catholics, the sacraments are the outward signs of the divine nourishment that sustains our spirituality.

* * * * * *

"Christianity born again" gives life to a spirituality that sees the beauty in the differences in people, not in their uniformity or conformity.

* * * * * *

In my personal living out of my life and faith, I have understood spirituality as the total response of "I" to God, to life, to others, and to the Catholic Church. It is that response which has become the total reality of the spirituality of "me." I do not believe that this is a negative form of individualism. I do believe it is a spirituality, not of a "born again Christian," but rather for a "Christianity born again" that is needed for the third millennium. It recognizes that the "we" in the church are different "I's" who believe in Jesus of Nazareth as the way, the truth, and the light. It is that recognition of the richness and uniqueness of our faith that make the People of God one. "Christianity born again" gives life to a spirituality that sees the beauty in the differences in people, not in their uniformity or conformity.

The very essence of a Catholic spirituality is intimately integrated with Christian faith in a Jesus who lived, taught, and asked us to follow him. With the words "Come follow me," he prodded us not merely to proclaim words, creeds, and pious exhortations; he was insisting that we must do as he did: All our actions must show love for all people. We must respond daily to the unconditional love that God has for each of us. If we follow Jesus, relate to him, and take action in the world with him, we come to know the "Abba" that he revealed is all around us.

This sense of a Christian spirituality formed within a true faith in the one and only true God was wonderfully captured by Bishop Thomas Gumbleton (*National Catholic Reporter*, October 27, 2016):

Again, it's not just saying, "Yes, I believe in God the Father Almighty," and we say "yes" to all those things. That's an aspect of faith, but it's not what we're talking about really in the Scriptures. Faith is how we relate to God; it's our relationship with God. Faith means that we trust God, we have confidence in God, we know God, and we know God knows us. It's a profound and deep relationship that we keep trying to build on, deepen, and make more real in our lives.

If we claim to be followers of Jesus, then how can we not explore, reflect, and imitate his life and actions? Isn't that both the spiritual and worldly tradition of Christianity? "The thief comes only to steal and kill and destroy. I came that they may have life, and have it abundantly" (John 10:10). This notion hits us even more powerfully when we hear this truth in today's vernacular as translated by Eugene Peterson in *The Message*: "A thief is only there to steal and kill and destroy. I came so they can have real and eternal life, more and better life than they ever dreamed of."

And let's face it. We don't all have the exact same dreams. "*Vive la différence,*" is what I say. Intolerance of diversity among religious people in today's shrinking globe breeds acrimony—not a holiness that promises a "better life than they ever dreamed of." Christian spiritual tradition at its core is our actions conveying throughout history the life, behavior, and love that Jesus taught and lived.

How simplistic and "unchristian" it would be to entertain the notion of tradition as a fossilized past that does not require an enlivening transformation to be relevant in the evolving now. As Gabriel Moran states in the epigraph to this chapter: "The proper attitude toward tradition is neither preservation nor rejection but to rethink the whole tradition with the help of present knowledge." And how on earth can a person or an institution—especially our worldwide Catholic Church—rethink Jesus' two-thousand-year-old revelation without asking questions in the bright light of a modern understanding of the world around us?

Is a conviction to "rethink the whole of tradition" a liberal view; a progressive view; a conservative view; an orthodox view? The answer to that question is: It is none of the above. Moran's view is clearly a "Christianity born again" view that must become the Catholic Church's view if we are to speak to all people meaningfully in the third millennium.

If we do not learn to view Christian tradition in the light of transformation, it will become a dead religion, perpetuating the attitudes, practices, and culture of people who lived centuries, even millennia, ago. We Christians would be compelled to worship in the temple. It would be appropriate for Christians like us to own slaves—if we treated them fairly: "Blessed is that slave whom his master will find at work when he arrives" (Luke 12.43). Jesus never ordained anyone, especially not just men, or consecrated bishops, or elected a pope. Should the Catholic Church only celebrate Mass in the evening, and never in the morning, since Jesus initiated the Last Supper—not the Last Breakfast?

Tradition, rejuvenated in and for the "now" is essential in order for today's Christians to grasp Jesus' revelations from the past. Those revelations are the essence of our Christian faith. But tradition must be understood not as a static remembrance of the past but as today's actions by Christians in the world who have been inspired anew by that past. As Moran so persuasively points out in *Missed Opportunities*:

> *A divine revelation is not a collection of truths that the Roman Catholic Church possesses; it is an activity requiring interpretations by religious bodies, including the Roman Catholic Church. In a religious use of revelation, the word can only function as a verb, not a noun.*

It is in our rich Catholic intellectual tradition, in which "faith seeks understanding," that we should realize that Christians must "do Christianity" (the verb) and not just "be Christians" (the noun). As a matter of fact, it is not enough for us to be "born again Christians" but rather we must experience "Christianity born again." We are called by our faith to transform the world, to act in ways whereby our Christian faith continuously embraces and renews an ever-changing world.

Anyone who is even half awake in this technological world today is acutely aware of the endless stream of new information, exploding at a pace never before seen in human history. A bewildering plethora of scientific discoveries and new technologies appear almost daily in every realm of human activity. But curiously—even astonishingly to some of us—many of our fellow Christians fail to see these advances as wonders of God, who created and nurtures all natural phenomena.

How can faithful Christians who are not dedicated to a "Christianity born again" expect to remain relevant in the new millennium? How can a Christianity content with "born again Christians," that rests on the laurels of past practices and time-honored, but perhaps time-worn, explanations of the faith, have any significance for the new generations populating the globe? Christians must, as Moran admonishes us, "rethink the whole tradition with the help of present knowledge" by causing Christianity itself to be born again.

Without equivocation Jesus tells us, "Do not think that I have come to abolish the law or the prophets; I have come not to abolish but to fulfill" (Matthew 5:17). Most of the practicing Jews who lived around Jesus could not understand how this working-class Jew had the audacity to question the orthodox practices and doctrines of those times. How dare he be so insolent as to question what the Temple leaders taught as dictums of God? They simply did not understand that Jesus was not destroying Judaism's traditions; rather he was rethinking Judaism for his time…and giving it a new birth for all times.

Perhaps we can better appreciate what Jesus was trying to tell the people in that famous passage cited above by studying Peterson's modern translation of Matthew 5:17 in *The Message*:

"Don't suppose for a minute that I have come to demolish the Scriptures—either God's Law or the Prophets. I'm not here to demolish but to complete. I am going to put it all together, pull it all together in a vast panorama. God's Law is more real and lasting than the stars in the sky and the ground at your feet. Long after stars burn out and earth wears out, God's Law will be alive and working."

Why are we Christians today blind to what Jesus did to and for Judaism? Why is it so difficult for us to see how Jesus transformed Judaism and pulled it "all together in a vast panorama"? Jesus was born, lived, and died a Jew. There is no denying that. However, it likewise cannot be argued that he was punctilious about traditions and best religious practices. He was not condemned to death because he was taken for a fervently orthodox, scrupulous, obedient, "born again Jew." No, he was scourged, humiliated, and nailed to a cross because he declared "Judaism born again." He dared to foment a Jewish renaissance, which eventually became what we know as Christianity, by announcing a new spirituality, in a new age, at a new time, and with new ways to imagine Judaism's traditions.

Listen to Paul in Galatians, from the translation in *The Message*. Paul startles those around him when he shouts out:

You crazy Galatians! Did someone put a hex on you? Have you taken leave of your senses? Something crazy has happened, for it's obvious that you no longer have the crucified Jesus in clear focus in your lives.

Galatians 3:1

Later in his pointed discourse with them he says:

Answer this question: Does the God who lavishly provides you with his own presence, his Holy Spirit, working things in your lives you could never do for yourselves, does he do these things because of your strenuous moral striving or because you trust him to do them in you? Don't these things happen among you just as they happened with Abraham? He believed God, and that act of belief was turned into a life that was right with God. Is it not obvious to you that persons who put their trust in Christ (not persons who put their trust in the law!) are like Abraham: children of faith? It was all laid out beforehand in Scripture that God would set things right with non-Jews by faith. Scripture anticipated this in the promise to Abraham: "All nations will be blessed in you."

Galatians 3:5-8

When we read and reflect on the life of Jesus as chronicled in the New Testament, we cannot help but see how this faithful and holy Jew caused turmoil among the temple leaders and the "faithful" of his time and religion. With his words, and by his actions, Jesus continually challenged and questioned Jewish traditions and practices. He argued with and questioned the temple leaders as to why he shouldn't heal on the Sabbath; he challenged and questioned a group of Jews who were about to stone an adulterous woman to death; he confronted and questioned the money changers in the temple, turning over their tables; he refused to follow the religious customs of his time by associating with sinners, outcasts, tax collectors, even gentiles. Such anti-authoritarian behavior was scandalous in those times. But that is how "Judaism born again" became Christianity. Now that Christianity, two thousand years later, needs to become "Christianity born again."

Jesus repeatedly questioned the existing religious traditions of "God's Chosen People," and he was the Son of God! Indeed, Jesus' own life clearly proves that challenging religious authority is not heresy. Questioning what traditional interpretation of God's revelation to us can be not merely acceptable but absolutely a necessity in living a faith-filled spirituality. We, as followers of Jesus, are called to understand our spiritual traditions, make them meaningful, and bring them to life in our particular time in history. It really is that simple. It really is Christian common sense.

And it is not heresy. It is not watering down or dumbing down Christian values, as some protest. It's not forfeiting Christian truth and morality. It is not some ideological culture warfare "to rethink the whole tradition with the help of present knowledge." It is the living, breathing, loving Christianity that listens to what the church calls the *sensus fidelium*, the lived experience of the faithful.

So, in my life, in your life, in our lives, it is not un-Christian for us to ask, "Do you really know what you are doing, God? We want answers." And know, "Lord, we may not always understand your answers, but we do trust you."

That's Christian faith. That's Christian spirituality for today's world.

CHAPTER 4

The Importance of Squabbling with God

· · · · · ·

Jesus gave us permission to be as close to God as he was, and we have his permission to share our indignation about suffering, we have permission to argue with God.... We have permission to declare our discontent.

REV. DR. ROBERT M. FRANKLIN, JR.

· · · · · ·

Certainly, Robert Franklin's statement above on having an argumentative relationship with God is, shall we say, a bit unusual and unexpected in most normal religious settings. Some may describe having such an offbeat familiarity with God as abnormal, bizarre, even outrageous. Yet, the Reverend is no flighty, whimsical, religious zealot. He is the President Emeritus of Morehouse College; Visiting Scholar in Residence at Stanford University's Martin Luther King, Jr., Research and Education Institute; Director of the Religion Program at the Chautauqua Institution; and has a Ph.D. from the University of Chicago Divinity School.

To appreciate the insight and depth of Franklin's remarks it is essential that we are first transformed in today's world by what we previously described as "Christianity born again." That re-birth requires a current Christian faith that understands the cultural and religious traditions that Jesus experienced, so that we may better be able to "rethink the whole tradition with the help of present knowledge." We should reflect on how that tradition experienced in today's fundamentally different world needs transformation if it is to be relevant in the now.

Given today's theological and historical research into the life of Jesus, it is clear, of course, that he was a Jew. However, he was not a Jew only in ethnicity. Jesus was also a Jew culturally, socially, and religiously. He was steeped in Judaism's traditions and humanly formed and nurtured within and by his spiritual and historical culture and the religious stories and practices of his times. Jesus was clearly motivated to action by the Hebrew Scriptures he often cited in his teachings. (See for example: Matthew 4:2-10; Matthew 22:42-45; Mark 7:6-13). It was Jesus the Jew who observed the Passover Seder in one of his last free acts (Luke 22:14-15). And on the day of his crucifixion, when Pilate asked him if he was the King of the Jews? He answered him, basically, "You said it!" (See Mark 15:2.)

It is important for us to look back at how the Jews understood their spiritual tradition and how they subsequently related to God as they lived that tradition. We can't even begin to understand Christian tradition (much less that of Judaism or Islam) if we do not first go back to the unique relationship that the great exemplar, Abraham, had with God. Abraham is the patriarch and the *father* of monotheism itself. He is the father of the three largest monotheistic religions in the world today, with well over three billion total followers. He was the person, at about the age of seventy-five, whom the God he didn't even know called to leave everything and travel to a future Promised Land, a place he had never been. Abraham trusted God so much that when God tested his faith by ordering him to sacrifice his beloved son (Isaac in the Jewish and Christian Scriptures and Ishmael in the Koran), he submitted.

God chose Abraham to reveal the one Divine Creator to all future generations. The essence of the spiritual traditions that have come down to us today—revealed, revised, and reborn as they have been many times over the centuries, are all based on Abraham's singular faith in one God of all.

It can be quite enlightening to revisit Abraham's relationship with the God who chose him: It was God communicating with Abraham and Abraham interacting with God.

I believe we can discern the spirit of this original encounter by reading Genesis 18. The passages in this chapter of the Hebrew Torah detail what can be taken to be one of the most amazing direct encounters of a human being with God. In the first verse we are told that, "The Lord appeared to Abraham by the oaks of Mamre, as he sat at the entrance of his tent in the heat of the day." Yes, just another day for Abraham. But then God comes to his tent, accompanied by two angels appearing as ordinary travelers. As this encounter unfolds, God informs Abraham that he and his wife will soon have a son. This was startling news to Abraham, since his wife, Sarah, was far past childbearing age. Sarah overheard, and laughed at the absurdity of it. But Abraham, who did have faith in the word and power of the Lord, later questioned how she could laugh about this inexplicable birth. This part of the story reveals the spirituality of Abraham, who accepts and trusts that God can work wondrous acts. He has faith in God's wisdom, even though he could not possibly have understood how such a birth might be possible.

This is far from the whole story, but it is a most revealing glimpse into the budding spirituality present at the genesis of God's self-revelation to humanity. As Genesis 18 continues, we find out that the two angels were on their way to Sodom to annihilate the city and all its people because of their gross wickedness. However, the faith-filled Abraham, who had just accepted God's incredible promise that Sarah would bear him a son, considers Sodom's planned destruction unjust. That's right; Abraham questions and doubts God's justice. He earnestly believed that Sodom should be spared. He thought that because there were good people also in Sodom God would be wrong in razing it. So faithful was Abraham, so comfortable and trusting in this relationship of faith, that he presumes to bargain with God. In fact, (using *The Message* translation for its fuller impact): "The men set out for Sodom, but Abraham stood in God's path, blocking his way." (verse 22)

So Abraham blocks God from leaving him until he gets some answers or concessions. And—get a load of this—he dares to say directly to God:

"Are you serious? Are you planning on getting rid of the good people right along with the bad? What if there are fifty decent people left in the city; will you lump the good with the bad and get rid of the lot? Wouldn't you spare the city for the sake of those fifty innocents? I can't believe you'd do that, kill off the good and the bad alike as if there were no difference between them. Doesn't the Judge of all the Earth judge with justice?" (verses 23-25)

What is truly unbelievable is that Abraham wins the first round of the argument. God says, "If I find fifty decent people in the city of Sodom, I'll spare the place just for them." (verse 26)

But Abraham winning that argument is still not the whole story. He doesn't stop with blocking and telling God that he "can't believe you'd do that, kill off the good and the bad alike as if there were no difference between them" (verse 25). He proceeds to sweeten the negotiation with God, asking whether discovering only forty-five good people would be sufficient to save the city. God agrees. Now watch this. Abraham sees that he is on a winning streak:

Abraham spoke up again, "What if you only find forty?"

"Neither will I destroy it if for forty."

He said, "Master, don't be irritated with me, but what if only thirty are found?"

"No, I won't do it if I find thirty." (verses 29-31)

We are entitled to imagine that by this time there might have been a little edge of annoyance in God's tone:

Abraham pushed on, "I know I'm trying your patience, Master, but how about for twenty?"

"I won't destroy it for twenty."

He wouldn't quit, "Don't get angry, Master—this is the last time. What if you only come up with ten?"

"For the sake of only ten, I won't destroy the city."

When God finished talking with Abraham, he left. And Abraham went home. (verses 31-33)

What does this story reveal to us about questioning and doubts in our spiritual tradition? It would seem outrageous for today's pious Christians to entertain such an arrogant dialogue with God—*unless* we lift the veil covering today's spirituality and "rethink the whole tradition with the help of present knowledge."

Early Christians did rethink the Jewish tradition, and today we do believe that Jesus Christ was the Messiah foretold in Scripture. Belief in a Messiah is a core tenet of the Jewish faithful, passed down to this day, although most of them deny Jesus was that Messiah. Those who came before us, who witnessed the life, the teachings, the suffering, death, and resurrection of Jesus, are the ones who at the time had the courage and, to my point, the faith to "rethink the whole tradition with the help of present knowledge." Those who lifted that veil of tradition then, and we who lift it today, call ourselves Christians. As Christians we believe that Jesus Christ and God the Creator left us with the Holy Spirit to help us each day to lift the veil, to uncover ever more completely the inestimable truth of Creation. We will never be able to fully grasp God's unconditional love for us and all of Creation. That is why Christians are on that unending earthly journey of becoming Christian.

As Christians we believe that Jesus Christ and God the Creator left us with the Holy Spirit to help us each day to lift the veil, to uncover ever more completely the inestimable truth of Creation.

Christian spirituality should stand as a megalith of immutable and fixed prescriptions, requiring no effort on the part of the faithful to confront changing realities. Christian spirituality is always being transformed by changing times. A spirituality for today's people must reflect humankind's current, deeper understanding of our world. It must be informed by new and better information available to us, and embrace—not reject—a steady stream of broader scientific knowledge. It is as if a veil—permeated and interlaced with a kaleidoscopic array of information—envelops creation. We need transformed spiritual *information* from our church that will help ignite our spiritual imaginations to be *in formation* afresh. We should seek a new spirituality with the expansive frame of mind we find in *The Message*'s wondrous translation of Psalm 8:3-6:

> *I look up at your macro-skies, dark and enormous,*
> *   your handmade sky-jewelry,*
> *Moon and stars mounted in their settings.*
> *   Then I look at my micro-self and wonder,*
> *Why do you bother with us?*
> *   Why take a second look our way?*
>
> *Yet we've so narrowly missed being gods,*
> *   bright with Eden's dawn light.*
> *You put us in charge of your handcrafted world,*
> *   repeated to us your Genesis-charge....*

Like Abraham, who manifested a magnificent spiritual faith and trust in God, Christianity today must reimagine, reinterpret, rethink, and recreate a spirituality in which a world of new discoveries emerges.

Only a spirituality that encourages and facilitates the freedom to be in open dialogue with a personal God in an engaging and down-to-earth way can be relevant today. These are times of growing openness, an information age where people all over the world have instant access to all the latest news. We used to get our information from daily newspapers, always a day behind; or from magazines we received a week later; or from our priests in the pulpit, but we had to wait until the next Sunday morning to hear it; even network television required that we wait for the next scheduled news broadcast.

Today, all over the globe, we have at our fingertips all the information we want, when we want it, presented by people whom we have chosen to hear it from. Whatever you want to know is available at the tap of a finger on a computer mouse, a smart phone, a smart watch, on Twitter, Facebook. And today's flow of communication is not one way. We can throw out any question we want and get almost immediate feedback from sources in whom we put our trust. We get information and answers to their questions on our terms. The individual "user" is now the ultimate authority controlling the flow of information and knowledge—not governments, not media, and certainly not the Catholic Church.

Information has been *democratized*. Information has been *popularized*. No longer is the flow of information controlled by secular or religious authorities—no matter how much either may try to censure it. Information is now within the reach of people all over the world who seek answers to their questions, struggles, and doubts. They no longer have to wait for any official authority to tell them what they may question; what they need to know; or what to understand as truth. *Infallibility* has been transformed, in the eyes of some, from a divine gift that a pope is uniquely blessed with, to a capacity permeating cyberspace, accessible to anyone. All they have to do is lift their finger and click, click, click, away.

This new idolatry provokes the need for a rebirth for Christianity in the third millennium. The difficulty is not so much in the way that we have all been liberated as consumers of information—that's largely a good thing. The difficulty is that anyone who wants to may now pretend to be a provider of reliable information—and that's bad. The church cannot afford to ignore this ongoing transformation in the way people learn about and come to understand the world around them. To do so will lead unavoidably to a church that is seen, especially by young people, as lacking relevance.

The church must respond with an attitude of openness to the plurality of cultures, divergent world views, and penetrating questions blossoming around us. People today are enlightened by fresh ideas and empowered by their new-found access to worlds of knowledge. It is no longer feasible to hope that petrified ideas from the past—however cherished—will engage and instruct them. I believe Pope Francis captured this dynamic when he said in his homily at the Mass for the Jubilee of Catechists on September 25, 2016: "God is proclaimed through the encounter between persons, with care for their history and their journey. Because the Lord is not an idea, but a living person."

We today are less disposed to relate to God as a remote deity, delineated by others, rationalized, obscured beneath an impenetrable core of time-honored doctrine and rote recital of prayer; rather we seek, and will find, our spiritual enrichment in trusting encounters in which we are comfortable enough to question and faithful enough to squabble with a loving God—especially when we don't completely understand what's happening in the world.

Back in the fourteenth century, in Canto III from *Purgatorio*, the second part of the *Divine Comedy*, Dante elaborated poetically upon the limits of human intelligence:

> *He is insane who dreams that he may learn*
> *by mortal reasoning the boundless orbit*
> *Three persons in One Substance fill and turn.*

Dante's artful poetry in *Purgatorio* seems to capture the reality of the Holy Trinity so much more meaningfully than *perichoresis*, the formalized theological doctrine of the triune God. This theological explanation of the Trinity confounds most of us mere mortals. It is described, for instance, by the notion of "circumincession," Latin for "to go around," a description of the internal procession of three divine persons; or the penetration and indwelling of three divine persons in one another; or a mutual penetration of three divine persons resulting in a unity of divine essence. I wish in no way to denigrate the essential role of theology—and our theologians—for Christianity. But these descriptors can't really claim to captivate the common man or woman. Most of the faithful are not academic theologians or philosophers with the intellectual tools to penetrate such logic. The good news is, we don't have to be. The Blessed Trinity is spiritually clutched in our hearts in relationship to our own inexplicable and awesome encounters with three Divine Persons.

I see a magnificent confirmation in this budding evolution of a new contemporary spirituality in the straight forward and magnificent life of a Haitian priest. In Marcia Ross' and Jeff Kaufman's documentary *Father Joseph*, we see a spirituality that is meaningful and effective in reaching people who suffer in abject poverty. The movie is about the work and actions of a Haitian priest, Father Joseph Philippe. What is pertinent and powerful in manifesting this contemporary spirituality is Father Philippe's reflection on how he relates to and depends upon God. He doesn't have some pietistic, celestial, syrupy relationship with God as he lives and works with destitute people. He candidly says outright that he argues with God every day. Yes, he argues with God. He claims to do so because he is impatient with God. He says that he wants God to hurry up and help these poor, suffering people. Then, he threatens God with a grade of "Incomplete" unless there is a speedier remedy. So, how's that for spirituality?

How much better, then, can we embrace those words of Rev. Dr. Robert M. Franklin, Jr. (quoted at the beginning of this chapter):

Jesus gave us permission to be as close to God as he was, and we have his permission to share our indignation about suffering, we have permission to argue with God…. We have permission to declare our discontent.

That's Christian faith. That's Christian spirituality for today's world.

CHAPTER 5

Don't Just Take That Log Out of Your Eye, Get an Eye Transplant

• • • • • •

*The voyage of discovery is not in seeking new landscapes
but in having new eyes.*

POPULAR PARAPHRASE OF THE WORDS OF MARCEL PROUST
REMEMBRANCE OF THINGS PAST, VOLUME V, THE PRISONER

• • • • • •

No matter what age and wisdom you have achieved, you should by now have considered that your personal spiritual life will benefit from a questioning, candid, and engaging relationship with God. But don't be surprised if you experience some pangs of guilt if you do develop a more assertive stance. You may have been taught that a combative relationship with God is abnormal, inappropriate, or even disrespectful. If we are deeply grounded in that faith, you may ask, how can we doubt or question our loving Creator? If you believe as I do, however, that at the core of Christian faith is an all-knowing and unconditionally loving God, then an inquiring relationship may not seem so odd. But if you only see what you want to see, or what you always have seen, if you look only with those same eyes with which you have always looked, you probably can't see that there's nothing odd about it.

Marcel Proust has an important insight for us if we seek to engage ourselves in the closer relationship with God of which I write. Before we can unveil that renewed spirituality, we really do need those *new eyes*. Proust's insight may be just another way of saying what Paul tried to convey in Romans 12:2.

Do not be conformed to this world, but be transformed by the renewing of your minds, so that you may discern what is the will of God—what is good and acceptable and perfect.

If it is true, as Nobel Prize winner Bob Dylan wrote and sang, "The Times They Are A-Changin'," then how we respond in these times can't rely just on past visions, old answers, and reflexive responses. People who want to make the world better for all do not succeed if they only *react* to past circumstances. After all, those past circumstances brought us to the present. No! We must not only react to the past but must *create* the future. And to create a transformed future it is simply not enough to do what we have always done, only resolving to do it better. No! Creating a new future will require doing things that we have never done, and perhaps never even thought of doing. The old saw may be true: insanity is doing the same things you have always done but expecting different results. If we are to have the vision to re-invent our future, we need new eyes. So for God's sake—let's get an eye transplant!

Perhaps Proust's new eyes are a modern twist on the Greek term used often in the Gospels, *metanoia*. *Metanoia* uses a different part of the body, the heart, instead of the eyes to describe a spiritual transformation. It is a change of heart and mind in a faith-filled person who breaks from sin and repents and is reconciled with both God and all other humans. In essence, it is a fundamental and total conversion that Jesus himself proclaims to those who have seen the light of faith. Valerie Schultz captured the subject beautifully in an article entitled *Metanoia* that she wrote for *America* (December 8, 2003):

> *Metanoia is more lasting than a momentary epiphany, more active than an intellectual revelation. Metanoia is a radical change of heart, forcing one to dig deeply. It is a prayer answered, but it requires a further*

response. The potential to change, to see with new eyes, fires the imagination, fuels the visionary and changes, the world.

If our spiritual life, or the health and well-being of the institutional church, is dependent solely on rote, formulaic prayers, or teachings and practices that have lost the power to engage the faithful, how can we expect the New Evangelization (promoted by the last *three* popes) to remain relevant in today's world? We wouldn't need a New Evangelization if the old one was working, right? How can we expect that the faithful will have a spirituality that, "fires the imagination, fuels the visionary, and changes the world" if all we do is what we have always done before?

The De La Salle Brothers, my religious congregation, are fond of saying that we are dedicated to "Teaching Minds and Touching Hearts." While the institutional church has proven itself quite proficient at teaching minds, that is not enough today. We also need a rich and relevant spirituality that will touch and nourish troubled hearts. We, the People of God, must effectively reach out to people's broken, suffering, questioning hearts, especially those who may feel marginalized by the harsh judgment of church leaders, both in the past and in the present.

• • • • • •

All people must be free to seek their own path to God, including each and every Catholic.

• • • • • •

I am in no way criticizing those who pray to God in traditional ways. I do so myself regularly and often. No one has any right to dictate to others how they should find and relate to God. All people must be free to seek their own path to God, including each and every Catholic. I do take umbrage, however, with those, whether laity or hierarchy, who are not sensitive to the faithful who have already found *new eyes*, who have developed a renewed and rich God-centered spiritual life away from—and perhaps in spite of—time-honored traditions. But I am also saddened by those with *new eyes* who, because they imagine they are unwelcome, leave the church. They deprive the People of God of the insights and practices of their new and transformed spirituality.

Many that I call "spiritual-but-not-necessarily-pious-or-even-religious" Catholics (which include a disproportionate number of our young people) have left the church because of some harsh criticisms hurled at them because of their views. Many left because they were branded with ignominious labels: intrinsically evil, disordered, immoral, unfaithful, selfish, living in sin. The accusers who hurl those labels at people justify their sanctimony by contending that they are only speaking as Jesus did. I ask, then, is "Let anyone among you who is without sin be the first to throw a stone at her" no longer a Christian truth? I suspect those self-righteous "label-throwers" are among those who most desperately need an eye transplant!

Perhaps you have seen people at football games and other events with a sign that says "John 3:16," referring to the sixteenth verse of the third chapter of the Gospel of John: "For God so loved the world that he gave his only Son, so that everyone who believes in him may not perish but may have eternal life." That seems like a true and comforting statement for all Christians, but some people carrying that sign are really trying to say "…and if you *don't* believe in Jesus you will *perish!*" What I think we "spiritual Catholics" should do is go to the game with a sign that says "John 3:17," which in the contemporary translation by Eugene Peterson in *The Message* says, "God didn't go to all the trouble of sending his Son merely to point an accusing finger, telling the world how bad it was. He came to help, to put the world right again." What a different feeling that verse has for young people today.

Together, as the People of God, we must all come together and start talking, questioning, praying, and, like Abraham, pushing God (perhaps, even, with some impatience) to help us "make the world right again," to see new answers and have new hearts. Pushing God very likely must commence with prodding ourselves and our church hierarchy to be less quick to label others as conservative, liberal, traditional, progressive, faithful, or heretical. Without that eye transplant, all we will be able to see will be the past footprints of a conformist spirituality, a church where doctrinal acquiescence and pious practices define who is holy.

Remember Abraham. He was no wuss when it came to his faith-filled relationship with God, but he didn't back away from asking if God really knew what he was doing. For today's spirituality to engage with today's real world, the church must reach beyond sentimental practices and comfortable rubrics. The hierarchy itself must get that the same eye transplant as we do, so that all Catholics may see the world through the eyes of St. Paul:

> *Even though I am free of the demands and expectations of everyone, I have voluntarily become a servant to any and all in order to reach a wide range of people: religious, nonreligious, meticulous moralists, loose-living immoralists, the defeated, the demoralized—whoever. I didn't take on their way of life. I kept my bearings in Christ—but I entered their world and tried to experience things from their point of view.*

1 Corinthians 9:19-22, The Message

If we suffer from spiritual myopathy, how can we hope to be a church that becomes "all things to all people" as Paul says in more traditional translations? I guess we need to ask Paul to be our eye donor. We need his eyes, for the sake of the gospel, so that we all may share in its blessings.

We must each of us accept, on our own spiritual voyage of discovery, an opening up of our imaginations whereby we may witness anew Jesus and his Good News, practicing a spirituality that engages people today.

An enriched imagination may be just the thing to give us those new eyes that are the essence of what makes us in the image and likeness of God. Remember, all the "people of the Book"—Christians, Jews, and Muslims—believe God created the world and all that is in it from *nothing*. God imagined the universe and then created it. Imagination has the power to bless each of us with what mystical religion calls "a spark of the divine," a spark that cannot be contained. The Temple leaders, the ruling Roman powers, even the Jewish mobs could not constrain Jesus and his message of universal love. Nor can the Vatican or a grumpy pastor.

That divine spark is God's grace in our souls. It casts a bright light on our faith and is capable of starting a conflagration of divine awareness in those around us. It is through the power of our imaginations, and with the grace of God, that we may see the Holy Spirit awakening in individuals and in faith communities a new freedom that may enkindle in them the unquenchable fire of God's great love.

• • • • • •

We are called to imagine into existence what Jesus commanded us to create.

• • • • • •

God imagined the light and dark, the sky and the earth, the oceans and the mountains, the flora and the fauna, women and men. All creation begins with God's imagination. So there is our clue. Are we not, women and men, all made in the image of a God, who is pure spirit? We may best reflect God's image in our unfettered human capacity to imagine. We are co-creators of the world to the extent that our imaginations create here on earth the unconditional love for all that Jesus taught us to pray for. We are called to imagine into existence what Jesus commanded us to create: "…thy kingdom come…on earth as it is in heaven."

Baby Suggs, the slave preacher in Toni Morrison's beautiful book, *Beloved*, said it so poignantly: "The only grace you will have is the grace you can imagine. If you do not see it—you will not have it."

Institutions and the people who shape them—secular, political, or religious—are today deeply entrenched in set ideological viewpoints. Especially in the media. Where we rightfully expect "broadcasting," we now get mostly "narrowcasting." A commentator's or an entire network's ideological viewpoint is packaged to validate an audience's prejudices, twisted into what the audience thinks they knew all along, and shamelessly presented as if it were fact.

We see this similar divisiveness among Christians and even within the Catholic Church today, where so many are acting as if "that we may all be one" means that "everyone has to be like me!" What kind of Christian spirituality was "broadcast" in a speech delivered at Notre Dame University on October 19, 2016, by Philadelphia Archbishop Charles Chaput when he proclaimed:

> But we should never be afraid of a smaller, lighter church if her members are also more faithful, more zealous, more missionary, and more committed to holiness.
>
> Losing people who are members of the church in name only is an imaginary loss. It may in fact be more honest for those who leave and healthier for those who stay. We should be focused on commitment, not numbers or institutional throw-weight.
>
> …If 'inclusive' means including people who do not believe what the Catholic faith teaches and will not reform their lives according to what the church holds to be true, then inclusion is a form of lying…. And it's not just lying but an act of betrayal and violence against the rights of those who do believe and do seek to live according to God's Word.

Where does this "do only as I say and believe only what I believe" spirit come from? Does Archbishop Chaput really think that his spin on purity of the church requires rigid conformity to his way of seeing things, and that that means the inclusion of differences is a form of lying? Do the archbishop's remarks portray Paul's spirit of, "I have become all things to all people"? I am not in any way accusing the archbishop of insincerity. In fact, the greatest difficulty I have with his remarks is that I am afraid he is totally sincere. How can such words and thoughts illustrate the spirit of the Good News for Christians today? Who in the world reads the Gospels and sees Jesus as some self-righteous and rigid dictator of laws and conformity? How many times must we hear Jesus condemn as hypocrites those religious leaders who tried to present God's love as legalisms we have to adopt before we get his message?

This self-righteous portrayal of Christianity is a perversion of a Christian spirituality not just in today's world but would have been at any time in history. It could not have been exposed as deficient any better than it was by Pope Francis' homily during Mass at Domus Sanctae Marthae on October 24, 2016, just five days after Archbishop Chaput's intemperate remarks. Francis said that God's law was not made "to make us slaves but to make us free, to make us children of God." The pope offered that hypocrites, in their rigidity, must have "something hidden, a double life," and warned us of "the disease of rigidity." Then he went on to say rigidity was no gift of God. "Meekness, goodness, benevolence, forgiveness, yes; but rigidity, no!"

So, for today's world should we favor a spirituality that is fashioned to encourage cults, or a spirituality nurtured in communion with and for others? If we continue to cast away those Christians who think differently from us, logic tells us that at some point there will be very few of us remaining. The logic of Archbishop Chaput, as he articulated it at Notre Dame University, engenders a misleading, dangerous, and irrelevant spirituality for today's diverse and interconnected world. Perhaps Albert Einstein had it right when he said. "Logic will take you from A to B. Imagination will take you everywhere."

We Christians must take Jesus' message everywhere on this shrinking globe of ours: "Go therefore and make disciples of all nations, baptizing them in the name of the Father and of the Son and of the Holy Spirit" (Matthew 28: 19). If we don't transform our spirituality soon, we will surely become a church of cults, each having a small shard of the truth instead of the whole, holy truth that is of Jesus: everywhere and for everyone.

Today's hubs of connectivity include the internet, telecommunications, airlines, and the media. No longer are we dependent on individuals to communicate one to one. Today a message, a fact, an opinion, any communication, may envelope our world in a moment, floating in the Cloud. New ideas may be instantaneously accessible almost everywhere and to almost everyone. This abundance of images and ideas ignites the world's imagination more potently than ever before. If Jesus raised Lazarus from the dead today, just imagine the way that YouTube clip would go viral.

The point here is to underscore that the church must recognize that traditional paths to spirituality are not capturing the imaginations of a majority of people today, are not reaching them where they live and breathe. This is especially true for young people, who spend much of their day interfacing with modern technology. It is technology that is firing the imagination of people across the world today, engaging them, teaching them, entertaining, proselytizing, and connecting them. It has become an essential tool in communicating effectively. To ignore this is to condemn our efforts at evangelization to irrelevance. I believe this strikingly important truth is summarily stated by Richard Gula in his book, *Reason Conformed by Faith: Foundations of Catholic Morality*:

> *Understood in its deepest sense, the imagination is not merely the capacity for frivolity, in an otherwise serious world; rather the imagination is the capacity to construct a world.*

Remaining relevant in the twenty-first century will require a difficult transformation in the Catholic Church. While we have long supported the arts, we have not customarily appreciated the role of the imagination in shaping an individual's world view. Our forebears considered intellect and rationality the superior faculties of the human race. Even as far back as the great Greek philosophers, this bias against the imagination was repeated regularly. For example, Plato, in *The Republic*, declared that the imagination (eikasia) was the least of the soul's faculties. He was wrong then, and we can see that he is especially wrong today.

For the institutional church, the traditional way of thinking, that reason and divine revelation drive spirituality, was the backbone for establishing moral norms of behavior. For the institutional church, the magisterium (official teaching authority) provides governance, approves the rationale, and is the church's human link to divine truth. With this approach then, a set of Catholic formal

doctrines evolved that require an acquiescent, even a resigned spirituality, largely dependent upon institutional judgment to determine orthodoxy. This may
have worked in the past, but it is definitely not working in today's world.

Modern technology has engendered boundless novel ideas and new information and is reshaping people's worldviews in powerful and lasting ways. This
vast influx of knowledge has ignited a transformation in imagination, aesthetic
sensibilities, intuition, values, and—ultimately—religious beliefs and spirituality.

Personal experience and relationships, whether real or virtual, are now
what the forces that influence people the most powerfully. Authority no longer
resides solely with institutional leaders and decrees. "Received wisdom" is no
longer so well received or considered so wise. The final arbiter of accepted truth
is more frequently the individual than any authoritarian institution. This is the
real experience for growing numbers of good people on the Earth. It cannot, it
will not, be stopped by traditional controls of any absolute authority, no matter
how hard it may stamp its feet.

That notion of Jesus on YouTube mentioned above invites us to imagine
Christ among us today. Jesus, the great communicator, who used the things
with which his disciples had everyday familiarity to convey to them his message of salvation and the power of universal love: the lilies of the field, wheat
and chaff, a mustard seed, lost sheep, fig trees, the power of Caesar, toiling in
the fields, the nets of the fishermen. But is that how he would choose to speak
to us today, in the third millennium since his death? Would he speak instead
of quarks and Wall Street capitalism, of organ transplants, of nuclear arsenals,
gender identity, our failing stewardship of the planet, racial animus, income
disparity, and unwelcome refugees? Who, we may ask, are the outcasts of our
society today with whom he would seek communion? What hypocrites would
suffer his scorn? Who would he drive from the temple today? These are questions that have the power to engage and awaken us.

We need to lift that veil of our church's past spirituality, recognizing that it
is simply not now capturing the emerging imagination of today's people. These
young adults, and even the not so young, may be as faithful as their forebears
and traditionalists of today. But there is a difference. Most of them have had
that eye transplant. They see the Jesus of two thousand years ago that tradition-

alists see, but the Holy Spirit seems to have intruded into their spirituality and unveils more of that Jesus, that same Holy One, reimagined in the bright light of twenty-first century sensibilities.

That's Christian faith. That's Christian spirituality for today's world.

CHAPTER 6

Delicious Ambiguity

• • • • • •

I wanted a perfect ending. Now I've learned, the hard way, that some poems don't rhyme, and some stories don't have a clear beginning, middle, and end. Life is about not knowing, having to change, taking the moment and making the best of it, without knowing what's going to happen next. Delicious Ambiguity.

GILDA RADNER

• • • • • •

What an unlikely source to use in a book on Christian spirituality is Gilda Radner, the famed comedian of Saturday Night Live, who died in 1989 at the young age of forty-two. *Delicious Ambiguity* is her intriguing description of her novel reflection on her life as it neared its rapidly impending finish due to ovarian cancer. Perhaps, it is no more bizarre than to source from more spiritually inclined authors, who might very well describe living out their daily lives as "Blessed Ambiguity," or even "Agonizing Ambiguity."

Whether delicious, blessed or agonizing, many of us would agree with Radner that life is about "taking the moment and making the best of it, without knowing what's going to happen next." How we live out that ambiguity is rooted deeply in our spiritual lives. The Christian faithful should embrace the future, despite all its uncertainty, not with trepidation but with confident anticipation. In our faith we search for meaning not only in our own lives, but in all Creation.

It is through struggling that we connect with life beyond our own; with a God who often seems hidden to us. Our human body, frangible and impermanent, seeks a relationship with a divine spirit that is eternal—that is, with no beginning and no end. How could stretching our finite minds around the unfathomable notion of infinity not affirm the ambiguous nature of the spiritual struggle itself? Yet, this human spiritual quest is not some absurd and irrational fantasy. Father Jeffrey F. Kirby said this so well when he wrote insightfully in *Crux* (October 15, 2016): "The truths of the spiritual life therefore, are not removed esoteric realities. They're tangible, felt, and sometimes more real than the state of affairs in front of a person."

What prior disposition we bring to that ambiguity is up to us. We alone determine the depth of our own spirituality. It is in that determination that we live either a meaningful life, filled with hope, or a trivial life, replete with anxiety. As paradoxical as it may seem, struggling with ambiguity may well be a graced way of better understanding holiness in today's world.

The first of seven key ingredients that need to infuse our church if we are to ignite a spirituality meaningful in our times is a faith-filled acceptance of ambiguity. With all the information exploding around us, with all the amazing discoveries of science (which are to be embraced, not feared and reviled), and with the democratization of knowledge, the path to truth is no longer so clear, nor so easily packaged, and not owned exclusively by church authorities.

We live in a world where questions abound, and new discoveries are constantly revealing the world to us in ever sharper focus. Received wisdom is no longer automatically accepted by most of us as having ultimate answers to all our questions. No longer do we expect to receive "the answer" on any subject from any single source. We no longer allow proclamations from others about the nature of our world to go unchallenged. Elizabeth Kübler-Ross quite perceptively remarked:

> *It is not the end of the physical body that should worry us. Rather, our concern must be to live while we're alive—to release our inner selves from*

the spiritual death that comes with living behind a facade designed to conform to external definitions of who and what we are.

The choice between hovering behind the doctrines and rituals offered by the institutional church regarding death and the afterlife or allowing ourselves to live while we're still alive is ours.

What is needed is not a simple societal transformation initiated and controlled by any institution, including the church. It is difficult for church institutions to accept that their proclaimed—and often cherished—doctrines may be ambiguous at best and unpersuasive at worst. A basic definition of ambiguity would be a situation or statement that is unclear because it can be understood in more than one way. In such cases inherent doubt and questions always prevail over certainty.

A story I heard recently from a friend who is a Catholic school teacher illustrates my point. Kathy has taught Catholicism to four decades of grammar school children, including preparing eighth graders for Confirmation. Recently she was required by the big-city diocese in which she teaches to take a refresher course in Catholic doctrine. The course was online and consisted of watching talks by presumed "experts" on Catholic teaching and then answering a series of multiple choice questions where only one answer was "correct," and all the others were "wrong." Kathy did fine on the test until she came upon two questions for which she could not guess the correct answer from the list of possible answers. One question asked what happens to our bodies at the end of the world, and the other asked what "Transubstantiation" means.

"I'm telling you, Brother Louis," she said, "that neither of those two questions have anything to do with my daily life or the daily lives of the children I teach. They were written by someone who claims to know the mind of God, but they don't. I'm perfectly fine with explaining to the children that what happens to our bodies at the end of the world is a mystery to me and we'll find out what happens then. Otherwise, I get silly questions from my students like, 'How old will we be when we get our bodies back' and 'What happens if you were eaten by cannibals." And as far as "Transubstantiation" is concerned, I'm sure if you asked 100 good Catholics what it means to them, you'd get 100 different answers. I just tell the children that when I see everyone in the church get up to go to communion, I know that Jesus is present with us in a real and special way. That is what "Transubstantiation" means to me, but that was not one of the four choices I was given on the test. So I didn't pick any of them. I guess if you think too hard about it you fail the test!"

We need faith to believe in God, because God's very existence (not to mention how our physical bodies come back at the last judgement or how bread and wine are turned into Jesus' flesh and blood) cannot be empirically proven, as we could prove, for instance, that H_2O is water. None of our physical senses gives us the capacity to place God before us. We need faith to believe something to be true that we cannot see, hear, smell, taste, touch or even prove by reason alone. Since no material proofs can possibly demonstrate the veracity of our faith, we naturally hear diverse and oftentimes hazy explanations, which are rarely acknowledged as such by church authorities. In fact, the closer we get to deep truth, the greater the shroud of mystery. But religious authorities of all faiths have an incessant drive to present everything they teach as certain, without admitting any possible ambiguity, no matter how confounding the ideas they wrestle with may be. It is as if perplexity were the eighth deadly sin. Or, as one theologian once said, "Atheists and theologians have one thing in common; neither can hack metaphor!"

Many institutional church leaders and more traditional Christians over history have become uncomfortable with imprecise and uncertain language when speaking of God and moral norms. They have no tolerance for ambiguity. However, we can see quite easily that as far back as Old Testament times, the Jewish people accepted ambiguity as part and parcel of their faith. We read in Hebrews 11: 1-3:

The fundamental fact of existence is that this trust in God, this faith, is the firm foundation under everything that makes life worth living. It's our handle on what we can't see. The act of faith is what distinguished our ancestors, set them above the crowd.

By faith, we see the world called into existence by God's word, what we see created by what we don't see.

The Message

Clearly a fundamental teaching of our faith is that we must trust in the One God who has been revealed. And how do the Hebrews know this? The answer: by "what we see created by what we don't see." Can we get any more ambiguous than to "see created by what we don't see"? That's their faith. That's their ambiguity. And it is also ours.

So ambiguity is embraced right from the start of Divine Revelation. This type of wondrous yet mysterious real life relationship with God is not only a part of Judaic-Christian tradition, it lies at the very core of that tradition. Yet, many of us still seem afraid of this kind of intimate "honest to God" communication that God chose to have with his Chosen People. Maybe Sigmund Freud was on to something when he observed: "Neurosis is the inability to tolerate ambiguity."

Even as science and technology open up our world, every answer we arrive at offers occasions for ever more questions. In our secular lives we have learned to be comfortable with and accepting of this ambiguity. We understand that further questions elicit deeper answers, which then led to ever better questions. How suspicious modern people have become when they hear dogmatic answers about God and human moral practices. Many, like my teacher friend Kathy, accept that there are questions about life and God that have no pat answers. I think my reading of the signs of the times was seen clearly and forcefully articulated by Cardinal Kevin Farrell, head of the Vatican's *Dicastery for*

Laity, Family, and Life when he said: "If you find Pope Francis 'confusing'—you have not read or do not understand the Gospel of Jesus Christ."

Why are church teachings so often confusing, even doubt-provoking, when it comes to unfolding the mystery of God, the meaningfulness of human existence, and the laws that govern moral behavior? Is there a rationale behind the supra-rational explanations often foisted upon ordinary Catholics? By definition God is *infinite* while we humans and the entire universe are *finite*. Finite is an easily grasped concept. We understand clearly, and agree upon, what it means, It signifies a sensible reality with limits, measureable in time and space. *Infinite*, a much more complex concept, invites a variety of philosophical, mathematical, scientific, and theological considerations. For our purposes here, I use a straightforward and more manageable definition. Practically speaking, *infinite* can be explained as that which is beyond limits and is not measureable. It possesses a reality outside of time and space, and therefore beyond our reach *both physically and rationally*. For now, we see the infinite only as "through a glass darkly" as St. Paul put it the King James version of 1 Corinthians 13.

Using that as a working distinction, we say God is *infinite* and is the "first cause" that, logically speaking, cannot have a cause; otherwise God would not be the "first" cause. God created the universe as we know it and all things in it. As such God had no prior cause that explains his existence, so we say God always was and will be, i.e. God is *infinite*.

Christians believe that God created women and men and are therefore *some thing*, a human person. However, we believe God as first cause is *no thing* (nothing?) which is why we say God is Divine Spirit. So, from *no thing* (God), we became *some thing* (women and men). Therefore, our spiritual life is always on a real-life journey (*some thing*) seeking the God of our faith who is *no thing*.

So, using the working definitions above, we can say that God is *infinite* and therefore cannot have a cause. Thus we *believe*, as an article of faith—but do not *know*, as an article of science—that God created the universe, including us, and that God always was and always will be. Anything more definitive than that is literally too big for our little brains to hold.

Robert McKim, Philosopher of Religion at the University of Illinois at Urbana-Champaign, delves into this very subject in his book, *Religious Ambiguity and Religious Diversity*. He writes about religious thinkers who characterize this religious ambiguity as "God's Hiddenness" stemming from the ambiguity in which God is mystery. He observes, "…God is hidden to a considerable extent from almost all human beings at almost all times."

McKim then discusses the significance of religious diversity's continued expression in a variety of religious beliefs. Different faith-filled believers see God, The One God, the Same God, differently. McKim cautions that this diversity of understandings requires that religious beliefs different from our own be accepted in a "tentative way." His conclusion in all of this is quite compelling: "The sort of belief that is appropriate, given our circumstances, will not be dogmatic."

* * * * * *

Ambiguity better invites the inclusion of today's young people, whose faith is rightfully embedded in a spirituality that is not constricted by a need to control.

* * * * * *

Many of our institutional religious authorities fear that to use such descriptors as "tentative," "diversity of vision," or "not dogmatic" when postulating their doctrines about God is heresy. That term heresy is from Greek αἵρεσις originally meant "choice" or "thing chosen" but it came to mean the "party or school of a person's choice" and also referred to that process whereby a young person would examine various philosophies to determine how to live. So ambiguity should be embraced by religious authorities. It better invites the inclusion of today's young people, whose faith is rightfully embedded in a spirituality that is not constricted by a need to control, or to claim a proprietary understanding of an infinitely loving God.

Many of today's youth, and again the not so young, have great difficulty living with a spirituality prescribed by religions that are the actual instigators, even if unintentionally, of antagonistic relations among people and nations.

Unwarranted claims of primacy cause much of today's prejudice, succor terrorists, and encourage armed conflicts. Today's major religions have so far proven themselves ineffectual in preventing this perversion of faith and spirituality. A spiritual transformation is needed in a hurry, and that need is one thing at least that is far from ambiguous.

Until we are able to transform the spirituality of the faithful within the various religions on this globe to accept the innate ambiguity within each of our respective religions, we will not be able to stop the insistence that "my religion" is the only way to believe. To this point, I am intrigued by Julie Gold's Grammy Award winning song, *From a Distance*. She wrote this song in 1985 when she was twenty-nine years old. The song was well received and has become very popular not only for its captivating melody, but also for its resplendent lyricism. As with all kinds of poetry, it might be prone to different, even conflicting (ambiguous?), interpretations. For me, Gold's words profoundly yet subtly expose the ambiguity that our modern society must live with; an ambiguity that, fortunately, does not have to divert our path into anguish or despair.

I recommend a close reading of the lyrics of this song in its entirety. But, for our purposes here, I cite a few of the closing lines of *From a Distance* that I believe convey my point:

> *From a distance I just cannot comprehend*
> *what all this fighting is for....*
>
> *From a distance there is harmony,*
> *and it echoes through the land...*
>
> *It's the hope of hopes, it's the love of loves.*
> *This is the song of every man.*
> *And God is watching us, God is watching us,*
> *God is watching us from a distance...*

These lyrics elegantly express the mindset of a culture that embraces a spirituality of life that thrives despite the sin and turmoil in the world: the faith-filled, who have the harmony, hope, and love in their hearts while the One God is watching them. Hope is our response to God's distant call into relationship. We feel the nearness of a loving God right in our hearts; yet, we see that same God watching us from a distance. What *Delicious Ambiguity!*

That's Christian faith. That's Christian spirituality for today's world.

CHAPTER 7

Please, No More "Body vs. Soul" Talk

· · · · · ·

We are not human beings having a spiritual experience.
We are spiritual beings having a human experience.

PIERRE TEILHARD DE CHARDIN

· · · · · ·

The Christian faith has taught us that we are made in the image and likeness of God, our Divine Creator. So our spiritual reality cannot be incidental to our physical existence; rather it is the combination—or better yet the oneness—that is the essence of who we are as humans. Our spiritual/physical nature defines our very being. It is not just a part of who we are, like a segment of an orange, distinct from the other segments of our lives. Whatever classical thought may tell us, we are not fragmented, with compartments of reality defined by their function: "body," "mind," "spirit," "heart," "psyche" and so forth. Modern thinking encourages us to consider ourselves, in all the complexity of our nature, as integrated beings. Why would God have denigrated our person with inferior and superior fragments? In us, God has created a whole—and holy—human being.

Traditional Christian philosophy, however, posits that we have two distinct parts, body and soul. The tendency for us, then, can be (and has been for many of our forebears) to presume that we are an eternal spiritual soul trapped in an ephemeral physical body. Yet Christian faith informs us that God created every single thing in the universe—spiritual and material alike—and that we humans are created in God's image and likeness. As a result, all of creation must be in intimate communion with the Creator, not just select "superior" parts. Our bodies, our minds, our souls participate in that intimate communion with God as an integrated whole. We should perceive our unified selves as actualizations of God's will. We are "body-souls"—perhaps two manifestations in the same person, just as God is three manifestations in a single divine reality.

I'm not saying that I can explain the doctrine of the Trinity! Just the opposite. I am saying that just as we Catholics believe—but do not understand—that there are three different "persons" in one God, so it must be (because we are made in God's image and likeness) that we too may have various parts or functions as human beings. But we are still and always a unified creature, not a "soul-in-a-body" or a "body-with-a-soul."

• • • • • •

We are still and always a unified creature, not a "soul-in-a-body" or a "body-with-a-soul."

• • • • • •

Why does this even matter? What's wrong with describing ourselves as some kind of spirit that inhabits a sometimes fragile, often sickly, sometimes (not in my case) unattractive body that eventually dies and, as we are reminded each Lent, returns to dust?

I'll tell you what's wrong with it. We Christians believe that each of us is created by God as one, unique, integrated "I." Since "I" share in some mysterious way with that divine image, then so too am "I" in some real, but mysterious way, an image of the Blessed Trinity, one God—not parts of gods. And by extension, the spiritual reality is that each of us, every unique person, exists in unity and not a combination of clean and unclean, superior and inferior, parts. The Chicago graphic artist, ISz, put it this way in his book of drawings, *We the (little) People*: "I chose my name and identity because it expresses that which simply 'is'—the immediate and active life-state and timeless connection with all things."

Science explains our world by drawing hypotheses, then designing and conducting repeatable experiments to establish whether those hypotheses may be considered scientific truths by all the world. The church has a far more complicated job in helping each of us discover spiritual truth and meaning. The church needs to offer us the means whereby we may come to a deep personal understanding of God's truths and revelations in our lives. We cannot just be told, but must discover through our own search and discernment, as Teilhard de Chardin, SJ, said, that "We are not human beings having a spiritual experience. We are spiritual beings having a human experience." There are no shortcuts on our journey to discover the integrated "I" and our relationship to God. Though we are joined together in a community of worship, if our discovered spirituality is to be meaningful we must walk each step ourselves.

Our shared "oneness" is the second specific ingredient I believe is needed for a spirituality to be relevant in today's world. The individual is one integrated and unique spiritual being, and so does the human race exist in another kind of "oneness." ISz expands further on this thought in *We the (little) People*:

> *It is the lack of oneness in global society that is the driving force behind my work. I am compelled to fill the void caused by the emptiness in the human spirit by creating a collection of visually disparate raw material with which the viewer can engage. Those participating in my imagery bring their own unique perspectives and can manipulate the many elements in my work in profoundly individual ways. In doing so they can begin to see the endless possibilities of who we are and what we can become. This experience will hopefully leave a spiritual afterimage that fades into a realization that we are one family in the vast universe, a universe only fully explored and understood together.*

The tired dualistic separation of "body and soul" or "us and them" does not capture the imagination of many of us today, especially our young people. It does not speak to the reality of our lives. Modern culture reinforces a much more existential approach, an approach of lived experience, uniquely embodied within each person, but at the same time shared with all others. This evolution in world view has made traditional Catholic intellectual approaches, like this separation of the physical and the metaphysical, seem irrelevant. Such distinctions no longer resonate with our experience, or with a sophisticated understanding of the world in the third millennium.

Most thoughtful people today do not experience a separation between our bodily and spiritual selves, nor do we experience alienation between ourselves and other human beings. There is no chasm, as was thought in the past, between the empirical sciences and the lived experience of the modern person in faith. There is no cause for war between true science and true religion. Why persist in the accusation that the world is too secularized? Why should our spirituality stand in opposition to material reality, to dismiss every advance in thinking as a "dictatorship of relativism" or "anything goes"? Such thinking does not resonate with a modern spirituality, which accepts an integrated approach as a positive thing, not as an enemy to Catholicism. While such an existential approach may not necessarily take expression as a formal religious conviction for some, it is a keen spiritual reality for many. It is simply, yet profoundly, a sense of "spiritual beings having a human experience." It appears that Chardin had it right in the last century, but the institutional church, instead of nurturing an open discussion of his words, silenced him. This did not help the church and its hierarchy to better read the signs of the times. In fact, it now appears that they misread the signs of the times badly.

The limits of science within this cultural change are astutely described by Dr. Paul Kalanithi in his heartbreaking yet beautiful book, *When Breath Becomes Air*. Kalanithi was a promising young neurosurgeon who died of lung cancer at the age of thirty-seven. He wrote eloquently and poignantly about mortality. Of science, he wrote:

> *Science may provide the most useful way to organize empirical, reproducible data, but its power to do so is predicated on its inability to grasp*

the most central aspects of human life: hope, fear, love, hate, beauty, envy, honor, weakness, striving, suffering, virtue.

The Vatican exists in a clerical bubble laced with theological and philosophical entanglements as the pope, cardinals, bishops, priests, and the few laypeople who work there attempt to prescribe doctrines telling us what it means to be Catholic; the rest of the laity and priests, vowed religious, and lay ministers, on the other hand, live and breathe in a world of daily struggles, trying to hold down a job, raising families, supporting loved ones and friends, and figuring out how to live Gospel values in a world that often seems turned upside down. The church hierarchy, with the best of intentions, attempts to reveal the Christian faith to people whose lives are vastly different from their own. Their explanations of the mystery that is Jesus' Gospel are circumscribed by traditions, practices, and canons of regulations that constrain their expression of those mysteries in a way that prevents them from truly reaching many of the faithful.

The bureaucracy of the church often remains far removed from the daily realities outside. History reminds us this is folly. The year in which I write, 2017, marks the 500th anniversary of Luther's Ninety-Five Theses and the nascence of the Protestant Reformation. I wonder what might have been the outcome for the People of God today if the church hierarchy in Luther's time had faced openly the very real scandals he exposed to scrutiny. The outside culture, the spirituality of the people, was ripe for transformation, but the institutional church either failed to see it or, worse, chose to ignore it. Luther was excommunicated, and the 500-year rift among the followers of the one Christ began.

Pope Francis captured the essence of my argument when he addressed the leaders of the Italian Church in Florence in November of 2015:

It can be said that today we do not live in an age of change but in a change of age. Therefore, the situations we are living in today pose new challenges which for us at times are difficult to understand. Our times require that we live problems as challenges and not as obstacles: the Lord is active and at work in the world. Therefore you must go out to the streets and to the crossroads; call all those you find; exclude no one. Above all, accompany the one who remained at the side of the street. The lame, the maimed, the blind, the dumb. Wherever you are, never build walls or borders, but meeting squares and field hospitals.

Persisting in the old notion that we humans exist as a separate body and soul—not one well-integrated, breathing, loving, toiling, laughing, sinning, praying, seeking creation of God—is a significant roadblock to developing a relevant Christian spirituality. This tradition of dualism is but one way the Catholic Church's teachings have continued to present God's creation to his people in antiquated ways, ways that no longer resonate with and awaken them. This dualistic approach of "otherworldly/spiritual vs. worldly/material" or "sacred vs. secular" betrays a subtle but insidious disdain for flesh and blood people, living their daily lives outside the sanctified circle of approved paths to God. If the church wants to better understand its people, it should reflect on C.S. Lewis' insight into our created nature when he said:

> *There is no good trying to be more spiritual than God. God never meant [a human being] to be purely a spiritual creature. That is why he uses material things like bread and wine to put new life into us. We may think this rather crude and unspiritual. God does not. He invented eating. He likes matter. He invented it.*

It is essential for the institutional church to examine itself and the ways it explains the tenets of our faith and treats people who make up the Mystical Body of Christ. It cannot present a meaningful spirituality to today's world if it continually presents Jesus and Christianity in a cocoon of its own manufacture. Synods, called by popes to inculcate a more collegial and universal understanding of specific issues, must understand that it is not only church insiders whom the Holy Spirit inspires. They will not hear of the lived experience of the faithful (what we Catholics call "Tradition") if they continue to include in the conversation only older, clerical, unmarried men. Offering a few token seats at the table to the laity doesn't cut it anymore.

A "holistic," integrated spirituality for all people will not be achieved unless we forsake the dualistic thinking of the past. While I do take umbrage with the abuses of ordination, including not ordaining women, I want to stress that I am not talking against clerics; rather, I am talking here of the totally inappropriate notion that ordination makes a man better than his flock, entitles him to special favors and privileges, or grants him immunity for misconduct. We call this "clericalism." If you think that I am out of order in my conclusions about the way this particular sin undermines the nurturing of a relevant holistic spirituality, I cite for you an observation on the dangers of clericalism by Archbishop Socrates Villegas of Lingauyen-Dagupan in the Philippines, a prominent and highly respected cleric himself. This is what he declared in a 2014 address:

> *Clericalism speaks of privilege, prerogatives, entitlement, and special treatment. Clericalism prefers sacristies to the slums. Clericalism is more concerned with embroidered vestments than reconciled souls. When we look back at the history of the Church, Church reform always started with clergy reform.*

Christian spirituality must be transformed for today's world. A majority of young people are no longer turning toward major religions, including Catholicism, to find spiritual meaning. In the United States alone, surveys indicate that around 40% of those under thirty years of age do not consider themselves to be affiliated with *any* organized religion. Should this not convince us that we are failing and must change if we want to ignite a "new evangelization" that is truly relevant today?

The renewed spirituality we seek will more readily take seed in a globalized world if we do not insist on seeing everything in secular vs. holy or body vs.

soul terms. We followers of the Christ are one in communion with all people because of our unconditional love for everyone and the magnificent diversity of ways we can express that love—religiously, communally, individually, and physically. So too must the church proclaim and nurture a spirituality that is not based on a fragmented image of personhood; rather it must be a spirituality that blossoms from nothing less than a moment of epiphany: an inspiration, a vision, a surprise visitation on a road in the wilderness. We must see humanity as one lovable, holistic, unique creation of God who, in communion with and supported by the church, is truly a spiritual/physical being.

That's Christian faith. That's Christian spirituality for today's world.

CHAPTER 8

Sensuality and Christianity—
A Combo Made in Heaven

• • • • • •

Our sensuality is grounded in nature, in compassion, and in grace.
In our sensuality, God is.

JULIAN OF NORWICH

• • • • • •

Sensuality and Christianity: For many, these two just don't seem to go together. The subject of sensuality is rarely broached within the church without apprehension, despite repeated doctrinal proclamations that sensuality and spirituality are rightfully integrated. The institutional church sometimes speaks on this topic, but there is a disconnect between what the church says scripture tells us, and what the church really supports in its pastoral direction regarding how we are to live our daily lives.

The reason for this? Sex. There, I've said the word, now we'll have to discuss it. Sex among humans is, if you will, the ultimate form of sensuality. It is the way that two people can relate to one another in the most intimate of ways. Now, there are many other forms of sensuality, from gazing at a beautiful sunset to enjoying a great meal of pasta to taking a walk through a world-class art museum. The word *sensuality*, of course comes from the same root as senses, of which most of us have five. So our sensual nature is an integral, and natural, part of being human.

Sex, on the other hand, is a form of sensuality that not all humans engage in. Some people are sexually inactive because they are too old or too young, physically not able to do so, or have not found the person and the circumstances that seem right for them. And some do not do so because of moral or religious reasons that they believe in and follow. Women and men in Religious Orders, like myself, and most ordained priests voluntarily abstain from sex in order to serve others better.

Then there are the matters of marriage, family, and children that complicate the sexual act. Sex is the way we humans propagate our species, and that is a very good thing. And many, but not all, cultures believe that sex should only take place between a man and a woman who are heterosexual, commited to a lifelong and faithful relationship, and open to and willing to raise children. This is the position of the Catholic Church regarding marriage today.

However, it is becoming increasingly clear that many people in modern society—including Catholics in the United States—accept without judgment the idea that a loving heterosexual couple can have consensual sex before committing to marriage. And it is also clear that people who have a different sexual orientation have sexual relations both inside and outside of marriage and are forming families and having and raising children.

What are we to make of all of this, especially in light of traditional Catholic teaching on sex and marriage? The answer lies in a better understanding of sensuality and the nature of love.

Pope John Paul II, in his encyclical, *Veritatis Splendor* (1993), refers back to the Fifth Lateran Council (1512-1517) in support of a holistic Christian anthropology. He declares quite forthrightly that "...the church's teachings on the unity of the human person, whose rational soul is *per se et essentialiter* the form of his body. The spiritual and immortal soul is the principle of unity of the human being, whereby it exists as a whole—*corpore et anima unus*—as a person."

Why then, does the church seem to support a culture that harbors spiritual elements as distinct—and of a higher order—than a person's physical, sensual, sexual dimensions? There seems to be an almost incessant preoccupation, often bordering on obsession, with people's very natural desire for intimacy and for physical relations as an expression of love. For instance:

- Celibacy is accepted as such a "higher calling" that canon law requires this of priests. Jesus did not institute this requirement. Is there something unholy about a married couple being physically intimate? If not, then why not permit priests who so desire to marry and do the "natural" and "holy" thing, i.e. get married and have sex? Pope Francis may be moving in this direction, if not out of conviction, then out of necessity.
- Catholics who end marriages and divorce with just reason, but then remarry without a formal church annulment, may receive the Eucharist only if they live together as "brother and sister." Isn't that like saying "none of this debasing physical stuff permitted between you two loving persons?" What gives never-married older males who made that rule greater insight than loving women and men engaged in wholesome and loving relationships? Do we really consider physically intimacy unnatural or impure?
- The institutional church teaches that LGBT individuals are "intrinsically disordered" and that any intimate acts between people of the same sex is morally abhorrent. Does not science convincingly demonstrate that LGBT individuals are who they are because that is how they were born? Did God make a mistake by creating them "disordered and intrinsically evil?" Of course not. The secular world and many Christian denominations are now accepting— no, welcoming—same-sex marriage, adoption, and families. The Catholic Church must do the same.
- To this day, same sex married couples and transsexuals can be and are being freely discriminated against and fired from employment at Catholic institutions. Is that an example of Jesus' love and pastoral respect and care?

Again, a lot of opprobrium from the hierarchy, and many other Catholics, stems from a long history of conventional thinking about sexuality often based on ignorance, superstition and prejudice. But a spirituality based on ignorance, superstition, and prejudice will have no success in the twenty-first century. If you don't believe me, just ask any young person under thirty what they think, and why they think it.

• • • • • •

A spirituality based on ignorance, superstition, and prejudice will have no success in the twenty-first century.

• • • • • •

Is it young peoples' fault if they find themselves struggling to understand church teachings about Catholic sexual ethics? Are so many lay people wrong in their perception that the hierarchy's attitude lacks a Christ-like inclusion of people in loving same-sex relationships? Do those same men (and they are almost entirely men over sixty) not, too often, stand in rigid judgment regarding the search for intimacy and a wide range of behaviors now commonly accepted and widely practiced: birth control, same sex attraction, divorce and remarriage, gender dysphoria, sex reassignment. Even physical intimacy in heterosexual marriages is still treated by the church with embarrassment, as if it were somehow shameful.

The incongruity between church teaching and the lived reality of the faithful is perhaps nowhere more evident than in the issue of birth control. Before Paul VI released his encyclical, *Humanae Vitae*, in 1968, a papal commission undertook a three-year study of artificial means of birth control. The commission was comprised of seventy-two experts from around the world: bishops, clergy, physicians, married couples. They advised the pope that artificial birth control was not intrinsically evil and that decisions regarding birth control should be made by married couples themselves. Despite that conclusion of the distinguished group, the elderly Cardinal Alfredo Ottaviani, the head of the commission, convinced Pope Paul VI to reject this advice on the grounds that it would mean that the church would have to admit prior error on the subject. Today, multiple studies indicate that about 90% of Catholics of child-bearing age not only use artificial birth control but consider it a blessing. What does this disconnect tell us about the rigid traditionalists in the Church and their incessant negative fixation on human sexuality?

The answer to this conundrum is to unveil the spiritual nature of the senses and build upon that understanding an entirely new approach to human sexuality. All too often, the church seems to promulgate a dispiriting polarity between the spirit, which it considers good and holy, and the flesh, which we are to believe is carnal and corrupting. The institutional church frequently appears to focus predominantly on sexual behaviors as the core failures of a sinful person. Certainly this does not nurture a Christian, holistic understanding of the person made in the image and likeness of God. After all, God didn't just create souls and then let some unhallowed secular mechanism manufacture the requisite sexual parts. God created us as we are. And, for whatever divine reasons, created us with different sets of sexual parts and different sexual orientations, and in doing so God created an aspect of our being that brings the blessings of comfort, pleasure, and intimacy into our lives.

So, it does seem strange that so many would view as startling Julian of Norwich's insight that "in our sensuality, God is." After all, she wasn't exactly a bon vivant of her time. She was a fourteenth-century nun, a mystic who was highly regarded—even in her own time—as an important theologian. Her words highlight the inconsistency the church of the Middle Ages espoused in its declarations vs. its actual practice when dealing with people's pastoral, spiritual, and sexual lives. Therefore, I see as necessary—if we seriously want to foster a spirituality for the world today—this third ingredient that (along with a welcoming of ambiguity and an integrated one-ness within and among us): a true and radical acceptance of people's God-given sexuality.

In today's more open society, an enormous catalog of scientific, medical, and psychological research has undoubtedly helped launch a profound revolution in our understanding of human sexuality. This abundance of sound information about the subject has made most people better informed about the wholesome and magnificent role the enjoyment of the physical world, including intimacy with others, brings to a healthy, holy, and integrated life. It enhances not only the individual, but encourages and strengthens enduring relationships of loving couples of all kinds.

However the institutional church may preach of its acceptance of this perspective, contradictions arise in the everyday world of people's very real toils and struggles. The church's actions just don't match their words. They certainly don't jibe with the explicit sensuality found in the Old Testament's Song of Songs, as translated by Eugene Peterson in *The Message*:

Kiss me—full on the mouth!
> *Yes! For your love is better than wine,*
> *headier than your aromatic oils.*

Take me away with you! Let's run off together!
> *An elopement with my King-Lover!*
We'll celebrate, we'll sing,
> *we'll make great music.*
Yes! For your love is better than vintage wine.
> *Everyone loves you—of course! And why not?*

Tell me where you're working
> *—I love you so much—*
Tell me where you're tending your flocks,
> *where you let them rest at noontime.*
Why should I be the one left out,
> *outside the orbit of your tender care?*

When my King-Lover lay down beside me,
  my fragrance filled the room.
His head resting between my breasts—
  the head of my lover was a sachet of sweet myrrh.
My beloved is a bouquet of wildflowers
  picked just for me from the fields of Engedi.

Song of Songs 1: 2-4, 7, 12-14

These florid Scriptural passages bear no semblance to the hushed and awkward way the church talks to us about personal intimacy today. The church seems biased towards an almost medieval understanding of sexuality, rooted in the fear and ignorance of that unenlightened age.

Church leaders seem to have lost touch with a spirituality that leads people to a relationship with God through, with, and in the mystery of joyful human sensuality. In fact, why has the institutional church never learned that its discomfort with sexuality contributed to the conspiracy of silence regarding sexual abuses perpetrated by an all-male, unmarried clergy?

James B. Nelson's book, *Body Theology*, offers a trenchant analysis of problems with the church's current approach. Nelson, a Professor Emeritus of Christian Ethics at the United Theological Seminary in New Brighton, Minnesota, explains that traditional church teachings about sensuality could be described in general as a "theology of sexuality." This narrow approach focuses on traditional ways of speaking about sexuality using scriptural passages as proof texts. A significant challenge of this traditional approach exists today as modern theologians develop a "sexual theology" to replace the "theology of sexuality."

Nelson describes this modern approach by explaining that these theologians ask, on a fundamental level: What does our experience of human sexuality say about our perceptions of faith—our experience of God, our interpretations of Scripture and tradition, our ways of living out the gospel?

Unfortunately, these disparate points of view seem only to spawn disagreement among the faithful and our leaders, not to invite an open dialogue.

We can hear early whispers of what Nelson calls a modern "sexual theology" as far back as the fourth century. In the middle of the nineteenth century, Alexander Carmichael (1832-1912) of Edinburgh started to collect the prayers passed down the centuries in the oral tradition of the Celts. This collection became known as the *Carmina Gadelica* which could be translated as *The Songs and Poems of the Gaels*. These prayers bear an almost romantic reverence for the goodness of life and the presence of God in physical creation.

Their prayers showed very clearly a spirituality that was clearly comfortable with human sensual appetites and their relationship to the holy. Many of their house blessings addressed God directly as they prayed for "plenty of food, plenty of drink, plenty of beds, and plenty of ale." Some of their nighttime benedictions asked God to bless "the bed companion of my love," while other prayers would ask for blessings on "virile sons and conceptive daughters." Then there is a direct sexual petition to God in a prayer by the fifteenth-century Duchess of Argyle:

> *There is a youth comes wooing me,*
> *O King of kings, may he succeed!*
> *Would he were stretched upon my breast,*
> *With his body against my skin.*

I venture to guess that church spiritualists of a traditionalist bent today would remain reluctant to offer any such prayer! If the church does not forsake its apprehension about human sensuality, it will surely continue to lose generations of youth...as well as older Christians (like me!) who enjoy a wholesome acceptance of the totality of who they are. The traditional notion that the spirit is more holy than the body no longer resonates in the modern world.

The shortcomings of that traditional approach are captured persuasively by Marvin M. Ellison, the Willard S. Bass Professor Emeritus of Christian Ethics at Bangor Theological Seminary. In an article in *Christian Perspectives on Sexuality And Gender* (Edited by Elizabeth Stuart and Adrian Thatcher) he wrote:

My conviction is that unless we can experience and speak of God's grace in and through our bodies, in and through our sensuous connectedness to all reality, we do not know God's presence and power. Salvation is necessarily concrete and of the flesh. I yearn for the kind of en-fleshing of Christian spirituality that encourages me to embrace more radically the life of the flesh. Nor is that yearning mine alone.

It is past time that the Catholic Church openly embraces the reality that sensuality is properly part of the historic spirituality of the church, even if it was often hidden or glossed over in the past. Ellison was quite right in seeing a need "…for the kind of en-fleshing of Christian spirituality that encourages me to embrace more radically the life of the flesh."

The hierarchy in the church today must begin to learn from the joys and struggles of the People of God and all people of good will, and not just rely on their own, often limited, sexual experience. The Holy Spirit does not relate only to them. All people who follow Jesus and those who love creation are filled with a spirit that seeks goodness and integrity in their bodily, sensuous, sexual lives. This awesome dynamic was powerfully described by a popular human-relations author and speaker, Shannon Ethridge, who challenges the young and old to lead lives of sexual integrity. She said:

Think of the spirit as the "energy" we're given as humans who are made in the image of God. Think of our body as the "conduit" through which that energy flows. Without the conduit (the body), there would be no way for us to experience that energy and let it flow from ourselves to another human being. But without the energy (the spirit), our bodies alone can't muster the human connection we naturally crave.

We must always remember that the truths embedded within Holy Scriptures reflect the experiences of those who followed Jesus. The Bible is certainly not just a book of specific rules and regulations; neither is it a book about "all you wanted to know about sex but were afraid to ask." Jesus gifted and blessed all of the faithful with the Holy Spirit so that we will be able to share our lived experiences with all as a community of believers, not as an institution of judgment.

That's Christian faith. That's Christian spirituality for today's world.

CHAPTER 9

A Little Pelagianism Never Hurt Anyone

• • • • • •

When God pronounced that his creation was good, it was not only that his hand had fashioned every creature; it was that God's breath had brought every creature to life.... The presence of God's spirit in all living things is what makes them beautiful; and if we look with God's eyes, nothing on earth is ugly.

LETTERS OF PELAGIUS

• • • • • •

Not unrelated to our discussion of the need for an holistic understanding of our body/soul existence to enable the development of a modern spirituality, especially for our young people, there is a similar need for a more integrated understanding of our modern world. The essential goodness of all creation, and humanity within it, is strikingly illustrated in Celtic spirituality, particularly in the writings of Pelagius, a fifth century British or perhaps Irish monk (no less an authority than St. Jerome tells us the apostate was "stuffed with Irish porridge")—whose teachings were officially condemned as heresy. The spirituality of Pelagius manifested at its deepest levels a profound embrace of the communion between God and nature.

I must admit to some trepidation in presenting this topic for discussion. Our self-appointed "Catholic orthodoxy police" (some of us label them, I confess, the "Catholic Taliban") may well accuse me, by association, of heresy. I'll press forward, nonetheless, recalling a pertinent insight from the irrepressible American statesman, Hubert Humphrey, Vice-President of the United States under LBJ who at various times in his life was a practicing Lutheran, a Methodist, and a Congregationalist. He once wrote: "The difference between heresy and prophecy is often one of sequence. Heresy often turns out to have been prophecy—when properly aged." The Pelagian Heresy has had quite a curing time!

We have scant historical information about Pelagius himself, though he is generally known as a learned, religious British lay monk committed to a Celtic spirituality. He lived sometime between the 350's and the 440's. His heresy lay in how he viewed human nature. Simply stated, he was accused of denying Catholic orthodox teachings about the ineluctable detrimental effects of original sin on every person. He was accused of placing an unorthodox trust in free will and rational thinking in achieving salvation. Though he did admit that the grace of God can and does help, his critics contended that Pelagius heretically taught that people could find salvation within themselves. This notion controverted orthodox belief about the indispensable redemptive grace of God. Although Pelagius' teachings were attacked at the Council of Diospolis (415), his teachings were then only declared to be unorthodox; at the Council of Carthage in 418, his teachings were condemned outright as heresy, and that condemnation was ratified at the Council of Ephesus thirteen years later.

As with all questions of dogma, especially any thought to be heretical, volumes of theological analysis are available for study. Without boring down too much into the theological controversy or the historical dynamics, I would like to explore the Celtic spirituality that inspired Pelagius' message and got him into hot water—or perhaps worse!—in the first place. With such a study, we may consider whether *Pelagianism*, long expressed as a derogatory term and still considered heresy, may merit some reexamination today.

Some aspects of Pelagius' teachings were most certainly misrepresented or at least misunderstood, and they remain poorly understood today. To this end, I have incorporated the research of the Rev. Dr. J. Philip Newell's book, *Listen-*

ing for the Heartbeat of God—A Celtic Spirituality, a rich source of insight and understanding about Pelagius and Celtic spirituality:

> *It is valuable to examine the earliest features of Christian spirituality in Britain not simply because it teaches us about the past and helps us to decide whether history has dealt fairly with the first British theologian. More importantly, it enables us to explore our own spirituality today, and to consider whether our way of seeing has been impoverished by the loss of perspective that existed in the early Celtic Church.*

We should consider whether some important ideas relevant to the development of a twenty-first century spiritualty were sacrificed to the controversy surrounding Pelagius, but of course we should do so with appropriate caution in challenging traditional concerns about his teachings. My hope is that when we discern the essence of what Pelagius was attempting to unfold about God's Creation—rather than trying to re-litigate the Pelagian heresy per se—we may unveil exciting ideas that can help foster a more relevant Christian spirituality for us today. Maybe we could best do so by remembering what G.K. Chesterton said about the danger of his becoming a heretic: "I did try to found a little heresy of my own; and when I had put the last touches to it, I discovered that it was orthodoxy."

We understand at the start that the ancient Celts' history is somewhat obscured by the mists of time. The Celts were a group of tribal societies who shared a culture, religion, and a family of languages, but were not a delineated nation with defined borders. We find evidence of their culture as early as 1200 BC, stretching from the Black Sea to the Atlantic Ocean. From about 750 BC to 12 BC, they dominated northern and central Europe. Starting in the fifth century AD, their lands were invaded first by Anglo-Saxons, then Vikings, then Normans, and finally by English and French forces. By the late Middle Ages, Celtic culture was shrinking toward extinction. Today eight regions of Europe are recognized as fostering vestiges of a Celtic culture: Asturias (northern Spain), Galicia (northwest coast of Spain), Brittany (northwest coast of France), Cornwall (western England), Ireland (The Republic and Northern Ireland), Isle of Man (British Isles), Scotland, Wales.

So, let us muster the courage to take on, in a straight-forward manner, the "Catholic Taliban" by revisiting Newell's finely researched and penetrating perspectives upon Celtic spirituality in general, and Pelagius' teachings in particular.

Some of the earliest infusions of a Celtic spirituality into Christianity appear in the teachings and writings of Pelagius. He described the core goodness we find in the created world, so beautifully, as "the shafts of divine light" penetrating the thin veil dividing heaven and earth. Pelagius deftly captured the spiritual imagination of his people as he elaborated his understanding that the beauty of God's image itself, although camouflaged by sin, can be seen in each newborn child. He taught that all people can be considered to possess this same holy image, because Scripture tells us we are made in the image and likeness of God. God's grace, he taught, can liberate that innate human holiness.

Pelagius' writings brought him into direct opposition with the prevailing (but relatively new at the time) church teaching that every child is born in sin. Augustine taught that people could be restored to holiness only through the church and its sacraments. This belief directly countered Pelagius' assertions based on Celtic spirituality. Augustine's spirituality emphasized the church as "holy" and the world as "godless," a viewpoint that clearly resonates with today's traditionalist in the Catholic Church who consider themselves the true (and probably only) defenders of the faith.

In 644 AD, the Synod of Whitby convened by Oswy, King of Northumbria (northern England/south-east Scotland,) commenced a diminishment in the acceptance of the still-vital Celtic spiritual tradition. (This synod occurred over 200 years after the death of Pelagius.) The Synod was called to resolve a divisive conflict between the Celtic spiritual tradition and the Roman tradition. While the Synod is better known for dealing with issues we might not see as of terrible critical theological import today—like the proper date to celebrate Easter, and the sanctioned way to shave one's head—the synod nonetheless represented a struggle for hegemony between Roman ways and Celtic, or Ionian, ways that extended naturally to important spiritual concepts.

The Celtic perspective emphasized the goodness of all creation, focused on discernment of the presence of God in the heart of every person. This line of thinking engendered sympathy for the particular, for the natural world, and for the everyday realities of life. It maintained that we can ourselves discover God's living grace in the tangible world. A resplendent iconic image captured this Celtic vision, and can be found in countless artistic depictions of a signature character of that age: "the beloved disciple," whose name is never spoken in Scripture, at the Last Supper, resting his head on Jesus' breast and listening for the heartbeat of God. Those who listened to Jesus' heartbeat, it was thought, would be blessed to hear God's love for all people, all living things, all of the environment, and all of creation.

> • • • • • •
>
> *The Celtic perspective engendered sympathy for the particular, for the natural world, and for the everyday realities of life.*
>
> • • • • • •

Yes, listening to the heartbeat of God! This vivid image within Celtic spirituality had deep roots within Christianity's historical tradition, originating with Saint John the Evangelist—considered by most to be the beloved disciple. (His six mentions of the never-named "beloved disciple" are repeated by no other evangelist.) This notion of listening can even be traced back to the Old Testament's tradition of Hebrew wisdom literature, which Newell describes as "…a spirituality characterized by a listening within all things for the life of God."

King Oswy decided on all counts in favor of the Roman traditions, fixing the liturgical calendar, assuring proper tonsures, and effecting the inevitable decline in Celtic spirituality. The triumph of the Roman perspective encouraged a spirituality that looked away from this worldly life and—through the church—toward heaven. It was quickly embraced by most within the institutional church. The Roman Church thereafter more sharply separated itself from material/worldly concerns and put an ascetic/other-worldly aura into its teaching and preaching. However, history clearly corroborates that the medieval hierarchy did not always match its spiritual talk with its own worldly actions and life-styles. Still, the Roman perspective overshadowed to a significant degree Celtic spirituality's emphasis on integrating our lives more intimately with the essence of God's innate goodness as found in all creation.

This long antagonism can rightly be thought of as a geo-political divorce between Celtic and Roman spiritualties. Widening the gap were the fifth century barbarian invasions of Britain and the 410 sack of Rome by the Visigoths. As a result of these invasions, the Roman army withdrew from Britain to return to Rome's defense. This caused a further distancing of the then-young Celtic Church from its Roman roots and influence. Without a strong Roman presence and influence during this time, Celtic spirituality developed and thrived in its distinctive form, but only in a confined geographical area.

Adding to Celtic spirituality's demise was the criticism of religious traditionalists of the time, who condemned the Celtic Christians' core vision of seeing the presence of God in all creation and all material elements. They derided this thinking as a form of *pantheism*, a belief that too-closely identifies God and nature, viewing God and God's creation as one and the same. Such a belief is certainly contrary to settled church teachings and is rightly considered heretical, even today. But what now seems not to be so clear is whether that charge represents an accurate picture of Celtic spirituality at the time, or was merely the rhetoric of the opponents of an unorthodox provincial spirituality in the far provinces of Europe.

Not until hundreds of years later, in the ninth century, did a more properly aged discussion of the topic begin, when an important theologian and philosopher elaborated once again on Celtic spirituality. John Scotus Eriugena (810-877), an outstanding teacher of Celtic spirituality, talked of Jesus wearing two shoes—scripture and creation. He stressed that we must find God through Jesus speaking to us in Scripture but also in his walking among us in the world, God's creation.

Newell in *Listening for the Heartbeat of God*, explains Scotus' Celtic philosophy: "...goodness is not an attribute of being; rather being is an attribute of goodness. In other words, goodness is not simply a feature of life but gives rise to life. Evil, therefore, is opposed to existence; whereas goodness is creative, evil is destructive. Eriugena insisted that nothing in nature is evil in itself." In 1225 Scotus' main treaties were condemned, and in 1685 they were placed on the Index of condemned writings, that is, forbidden to even be read by Catholics.

But now, as Pelagius' heresy has had even more time to "properly age," perhaps we can acknowledge that it may not be heresy itself to simply place a 600-year-old heresy under a modern microscope and observe whether non-heretical lessons might be drawn from that examination.

• • • • • •

The consequences of our disregard for our natural environment fall especially upon the marginalized and downtrodden.

• • • • • •

Around the world, people today continue to express a growing concern about our responsibilities toward our planet. Core images of Celtic spirituality—like those shafts of divine light penetrating the thin veil dividing earth and heaven—may offer an abundance of opportunities to fire twentieth century imaginations bent on living in harmony with nature. Witness the growing animus toward industries and nations that abuse nature, who desecrate God's creation. The international impetus to stop humankind's disruption of the climate and curb pervasive environmental abuses seems to grow every day.

The consequences of our disregard for our natural environment fall especially upon the marginalized and downtrodden. The poor, in their abject poverty, lack power, sometimes even a voice, in defense of their own health. We need look no further than the drinking water of Flint, Michigan, to see the soulless devastation wreaked by bureaucrats who have lost all sense of our spiritual connection to the resources of this created earth.

We should fully embrace our responsibilities to our natural environment and fan the fire that Pope Francis ignited in expressing his concern for the created world we live in—resonant as it is with the spirit of a Celtic spirituality. That rhetorical fire burns beautifully as it was presented in Pope Francis' encyclical, *Laudato Si', On Care for Our Common Home,* and in his reflection on Saint Francis' vision for the integrity of God's creation. No matter what our religion, nationality, political affiliation, or economic status, we should join in universal appreciation of Saint Francis' canticle, with which Pope Francis starts this encyclical.

> *Laudato si', mi' Signore —praise be to you, my Lord.... Praise be to you, my Lord, through our sister, Mother Earth, who sustains and governs us, and who produces various fruit with colored flowers and herbs.*

Indeed, we are gripped with the beauty of Saint Francis' poetic commentary on the essential goodness within all of creation. (Do I catch a whiff of *Pelagianism?*) If we read just the *facts of the times,* perhaps a lot easier to agree upon than the *signs of the times,* we all must admit our planet is ailing. Ironically, Saint Francis is said to have written these beautiful words in 1224 while he was in San Damiano, near Rome, recovering from a serious illness of his own. Today, our globe is inflicted and diseased with the sores of environmental abuses; with the scars from a pandemic of poverty all across the world; with internecine quarrels, many fueled by religious fundamentalists' intolerance for others; with systemic mistreatment of others because of their race, class, gender, lifestyle, or religious beliefs—always proclaimed, of course, in the name of economic good.

The world today, its nations, churches, leaders, and followers alike, must heed Saint Francis' inspiring exhortation that poetically embraces the harmony in God's creation. An inestimably achievable means of accomplishing such a holy endeavor will be to nurture a Celtic spirituality that today's world can understand and embrace. I believe such a possibility requires that the church cease its ideologically driven approach and provide new leadership for the renewal of our stewardship of the Earth. Indeed, the church has had centuries to "properly age" these ancient ideas. Can't we finally integrate them as our fourth critical ingredient in a living spirituality for today?

There is no need—nor do I have the desire or the skill—to controvert each abstruse theological argument about the heresies attributed to *Pelagianism*; rather, let us seize the core truths found within Celtic spirituality. That is what will speak to today's world. The Church must help the world to listen to that same *heartbeat of God* that the beloved disciple heard as he rested his head on Jesus' chest at the Last Supper. Such inspired and grace-filled listening will free us all to see the goodness and beauty that is in the very heart of God's enthralling creation.

I am convinced that Pope Francis is the leader who can set, and is setting, the stage for a new and dynamic Catholic spirituality. Of course, as with any institutional transformation, he is encountering resistance. That resistance must not prevail. Our church must overwhelmingly engender in our lives the will to follow Jesus with love, not with ideologies and rules. That is how we will be able at last to hear the heartbeat of God. The spirituality that will flourish among today's young people is not a set of rigid proclamations of distant authority. Pope Francis put it so clearly in an interview in November 2016, speaking of his newly published collection of homilies from his time as the Archbishop of Buenos Aires:

> *Sometimes I've found myself in front of people who are too strict, who have a rigid attitude. And I wonder: How come such a rigidity? Dig, dig, this rigidity always hides something: insecurity, sometimes even more…. Rigidity is defensive. True love is not rigid.*

That's Christian faith. That's Christian spirituality for today's world.

CHAPTER 10

Discrimination Against Women Is Spiritual Sabotage

• • • • • •

It cannot be denied that hardly any major institution in Western democratic countries treats dissenters and critics within its own ranks so inhumanely. And none of them discriminates so strongly against women, for example, by prohibiting birth control, by forbidding priests to marry, by prohibiting the ordination of women. No other institution polarizes society and politics on issues such as homosexuality, stem cell research, abortion, assisted suicide, and the like. And while Rome no longer dares to proclaim infallible doctrines formally, it still envelops all of its doctrinal pronouncements with an aura of infallibility, as though the pope's words were a direct expression of God's will or Christ's voice.

HANS KÜNG

• • • • • •

The epigraph above, from the controversial priest and theologian Hans Küng's 2013 book, *Can We Save the Catholic Church?*, hit like a bombshell and shook up many inside and outside the Catholic Church. For some this salvo was a burst that the church needed in order to shake up an ingrained institutional bias against women. Of course, for others this was just another instance of bombast from a way-out, confused progressive who has no business even claiming he is still part of the Catholic Church.

This was far from the first controversial opinion expressed by Küng. He is in no way the darling of traditionalist Catholics. In fact, for most of his professional life he has been forbidden to teach in Catholic educational institutions. He played a major role in an advisory capacity at Vatican II, which has not endeared him to the rigidly orthodox. In the same book he contends that today's Church is suffering from a crisis of credibility as a result of its own actions. He opines that the crisis is not caused by outside enemies as much as by its own leaders' lack of pastoral sensitivities for the People of God and by their repeated failure to read the signs of the times.

Conservative Catholics, a class with whom I long identified, and who are still my brothers and sisters, have failed to grasp that a spirituality that worked in the past is failing people in the present. The current discord in the church will be hard enough to resolve to the satisfaction of all, but if a sense of Catholic spirituality it is not articulated with Christian sensitivity and a sense of inclusiveness, it will not just be flawed, it will obsolesce. Young Catholics, many of whom I have taught over the years, have taught me this in turn, and the lessons were painful. But here I am now, saying what I believe needs to be said.

Whether or not we agree with Küng's observations is not the point here. The issues he raises are of such profound importance to the future of the church that they demand serious consideration by all the faithful. Discrimination against women by the church is not merely a matter of breaking the "glass ceiling," as it has been in most secular organizations. For the church it involves nothing less than articulating our understanding of our relationship with God—individually and communally—for both women and men, equally and together. The church's treatment of women is not a women's issue. It's a people's issue. It's a justice issue. It's a Christian issue.

The 1976 Vatican document *Inter Insigniores* blatantly asserts the absolute impossibility of the Church ordaining females because they lack a natural resemblance to the male Jesus. In today's world that statement looks as outdated and misguided as the church's ancient insistence, contrary to indisputable evidence, that the earth was the center of the universe. ("And yet it moves," Galileo is said to have muttered just after recanting the Copernican heresy, under threat of torture, in 1633.)

How gratified Galileo's disquieted spirit must have felt when the Pontifical Academy of Sciences affirmed in 1992, after a 13-year investigation, that the earth, in fact, does orbit the sun and always has. I guess the institutional church does not see the natural resemblance of women, who Scripture affirms were also made in the image and likeness of God, to the "person" Jesus. Pope John Paul II in his 1994 Apostolic Letter, *Ordinatio Sacerdotalis*, contended that this exclusion of women from ordination to the priesthood should not be considered discrimination, but rather, "... it is to be seen as the faithful observance of a plan to be ascribed to the wisdom of the Lord of the universe." Is this to say that the Lord's wisdom subscribes to discrimination against women? Obviously not. But what does this papal way of thinking say about Catholic spirituality to all the people of the world today? Will the women of our church have to wait another 350 years, as Galileo did, before we all recognize the indisputable evidence, the signs of our times, that women are in no way inferior to men, including when it comes to the seven sacraments?

Discrimination against women in the church is not a matter of concern for women alone; and bringing it to an end is just as essential for the completeness and spirituality of men as it is for our female counterparts. An objective observer, knowing nothing prior of the church, who took a look its structure and organization could only conclude that the phrase "People of God" would be more honestly reflected with the descriptor "Men of God!" Jesus told us to love our neighbors as ourselves. He did not equivocate between a male neighbor and a female neighbor. For example, the woman at the well in the Gospel of John clearly became an apostle to her Samaritan townspeople once she came to realize that Jesus had "living water" for anyone who would ask for it. Or, why are we so often reminded that only men attended the Last Supper, but not that the male apostles cowered and fled from the crucifixion, while women (and according to John, the lone beloved disciple) attended to the suffering Jesus? Why do we not proclaim Mary Magdalene as Christ's own choice as the first evangelist, the first to proclaim the good news of his resurrection?

• • • • • •

The fifth critical ingredient for a relevant spirituality for today's world is the end of the discrimination, and sometimes outright misogyny against more than half the human race.

• • • • • •

Clearly, we cannot attribute to God any suggestion that physical differences between our neighbors make a man or a woman any less a spiritual being than any other, capable of serving God in the church and in the world.

That is why I insist that the fifth critical ingredient for a relevant spirituality for today's world is the end of the discrimination—and sometimes outright misogyny—against more than half the human race. It's about time we become the all-inclusive community that Jesus proclaimed and stop nurturing the spiritual sabotage of Christianity with an indefensible doctrine that doesn't even meet the test of common sense, much less an "infallible" teaching of the Catholic Church.

We Catholics should never tolerate—in any secular organization, much less in the church—an unequal status for women. Do we really believe women and men are both created in God's image and likeness? Then that belief must take us beyond pious, paternalistic exhortations and be reflected in our daily lives and our institutional church practices. We simply have to put an end to the convoluted and completely unpersuasive theological rationalizations that to justify the hopelessly flawed ontological fallacy that women are not equal to men. They are. You know it. I know it. The popes know it. And all the defenders of the status quo know it. By whose authority do we deem the subjugation of women, routine in ancient times, to be somehow blessed by God?

As I pointed out in my book *Flying in the Face of Tradition*, the Catholic Church—as opposed to most of our Protestant brethren—believe there are two sources of divine revelation: the Scriptures and Tradition. Tradition can be simply defined as "the lived experience of the faithful," that is, we believe God's revelation did not end with the last words of the Book of Revelation. It continues today in how believers in the message of Jesus of Nazareth learn the truth about God as we attempt to live out his mission to help create the reign of God "on Earth, as it is in Heaven."

Let me give you an example of how Tradition works. At some point in the church's 2000+ year history, it became clear that there were times that communion could not be taken with both bread and wine. Perhaps it was during one or more of the plagues in the Middle Ages, or perhaps it had something to do with the effects of alcohol on certain people. So in its wisdom, listening to the signs of the times and the lived experience of the faithful, the church taught that either the bread or the wine could be consumed and the communicant would receive both the "body and blood" of Christ. At the time, it was an obvious, common sense solution to a real problem. This communion under one species became the norm in the Catholic Church for centuries, until finally the Second Vatican Council brought the practice of receiving both bread and wine back into common practice. But note that the church never said it made a mistake or was unfaithful to the magisterium either way. So even today, Catholics always have a choice of receiving just the bread or just the wine or both…for whatever reason they might choose.

Jesus didn't say we could take either the bread or the wine. In fact, he said quite directly that we should do both! But Jesus didn't know about germs or maybe even alcoholism, and so his followers were left to figure out what was the essence of what he was teaching and what was not.

Ordaining women would fall under the same category. First of all, Jesus did not exactly "ordain" anyone—at least not in the way we do it today, after a long period of discernment and study. And Jesus worked with what he had and in the society in which he lived. So he ordained only Jewish men! At first, his disciples followed his lead on this, but soon they realized that there were other people who were being called to serve the entire church community, and so they chose and then "ordained" some of them as deacons. It is now historically clear, thanks to the scholarly research of Phyllis Zagano and others, that both men and women were ordained as deacons in the early church. Over the centuries, the church, led by our Protestant brethren, has realized that Jesus could not possibly have meant that only men could or should be ordained, either as deacons or as priests—or as bishops, cardinals, and popes for that matter. Jesus was the original feminist. He had to be, if he was to be true to his Father, and there is absolutely no reason that the church cannot and should not follow this thinking to its logical conclusion: Women priests might not be in the Bible, but there is nothing stopping the church from ordaining them now.

I am serious about this. The debate is over, in my mind. If the Catholic Church does not ordain women, and soon, then it will not be seen by most of the faithful as the true church of our founder, Jesus Christ.

Before I am tarred, feathered, and driven out of town, let me just point out the fallacies put forth by those opposed to women's ordination. For some of them, twisted rationalizations of "complementarity" drive them toward garbled conclusions. But no honest reasoning can allow us to conclude that because we exist as different sexes, one must be superior and one inferior. God did not create women and men with obstacles preventing either from truly representing Jesus, or establish rules and regulations limiting women's role in his—not our—church. A woman can represent Jesus just as well as a man because women, men, and the human Jesus are all divinely created persons. Let's not forget, the church's own doctrine of the Trinity is expressed as three "equal" Divine Persons, i.e. one same equal divine nature yet three distinct persons. And, we see as God's image and likeness, women and men, i.e. the same "one and equal" human nature, yet two distinct gendered persons.

Of course, there are differences between men and women. But the church must stop using the differences God chose for us as a reason to discriminate. How could an unconditionally loving God create those beautiful and complementary differences to allow us to discriminate, one against the other? And let's please, please drop the specious argument that women cannot be ordained because they must stand in for Christ, and Jesus was a man and so must they be. The priest-standing-for-Christ is true, but it is a metaphor, for Christ's sake! Literally.

This may sound like an overly harsh indictment; but if we reflect honestly on plain facts in church history we see undeniable signs of an embedded institutional bias against women. To see that this is true we need only read the reflections about women by one of the greatest Doctors of the Church, Saint Thomas Aquinas (1225-1274). In his masterpiece *Summa Theologica*, still studied and revered today, we read Thomas' teaching on this topic:

> *It was necessary for woman to be made, as the Scripture says, as a 'helper' to man; not, indeed, as a helpmate in other works, as some say, since man can be more efficiently helped by another man in other works; but (by woman) as a helper in the work of generation.… Woman is naturally subject to man, because in man the discretion of reason predominates.…*
>
> *In natural function, the female is an accidental male, since the active male seed means to produce a perfect image of itself; but if a female results, it is because there was lessened effect in the active seed, or because there was some inadequacy in the matter, or because of some interference by an external cause, like the humidity of the south winds.*

Part 1, question 92, article 1 ad1

I do not intend to imply that most people in the church today would accept the notion that women are "accidental" males. ("Accidental" has been variously translated as "defective" or "misbegotten" over the years, but all of that is silliness. Thomas was simply wrong on this.) The fundamental premise in the second paragraph above, that the male seed seeks to create another male, is hilarious if we possess even the most rudimentary understanding of genetics. Still, it is true that Pope Leo XIII's encyclical *Aeterni Patris* (1879) required that Thomas Aquinas' writings, including this passage, be taught in all seminaries.

The following year Pope Leo proclaimed him Patron of Catholic Schools. Okay. I'll buy that, but even Aquinas, like Homer, nodded once in a while.

The point here that I believe is important for us recognize is that past writings, even of great Catholic thinkers, must be subject to review as irrefutable new knowledge evolves. Must it not be equally true also that the church is compelled to change its doctrines as new understandings of God's world evolve? But hidden bias lingers despite controverting facts—however beyond rational debate they may be.

The task of the church in teaching us is not an easy one. The church naturally relies on Scripture and Tradition as its sources of truth. As Catholics we believe that the church's teaching, guided by the Holy Spirit, flows through the magisterium of the church—not locked with the past in isolation, but as it listens to the lived experience of the faithful. Moral and religious truths, and the practices they drive, must necessarily be understood within a context of continuously changing cultures. There are many good reasons why we no longer enslave others, or stone adulteresses, or burn heretics and witches at the stake. As times change God grants us a fuller understanding of creation. Our response in faith must grow with that new understanding.

Throughout history the community of believers has encountered new realities that engender new questions, new questions that challenge old, often ineffective or plainly wrong, ideas. God's revelation continues through history, and the church must engage in dialogue with its people. It is only the lived experience of the faithful that will guide us in our search for a twenty-first-century spirituality relevant to our lives. Culture, knowledge, science, experience, wisdom are the ways God touches our lives, and they are not static historical artifacts. They breathe and grow as we breathe and grow.

Anyone half-awake understands that our lived reality is not some mere repetition of what has always been. In our lifetime, we have witnessed an awakening about the role and the rightful status of women in the world and in the church. Looking around the globe, we cannot ignore the sea change in the socio-economic and cultural realms—the sunset of patriarchal dominance—and we as Christians have to get out in front of the changes that has caused and will continue to cause.

We are clearly, in the late twentieth and early twenty-first centuries, experiencing a moment of epiphany (which means a revelation) about women. As ought to be expected with any paradigm shift, this change will be met by stiff resistance from those who were empowered by paradigms of the past, including some of those in charge of the institutional church. A woman friend of mine even asserts that conflicts exploding across the Mideast today may be less about religious fundamentalism than about a death struggle against modern culture's tendency to refute male hegemony.

• • • • • •

What are the institutional church, the hierarchy, and the magisterium waiting for?

• • • • • •

Fundamental changes to our view of the world are always controversial and downright upsetting to many. It is especially alarming to many organized religions, including the Catholic Church. Some people remain impervious to this shift. In their view, patriarchal dominance is not just an historical reality whose time has come to pass. They are convinced it is nothing less than the divinely blessed ordering of the world. But they are wrong.

How has it remained even remotely possible for institutional church leaders to ignore the very real and important sexual revolution? The faithful—men and women alike—have discerned the Holy Spirit's undiscriminating presence in the world of their lived reality in the here and now. My emphatic and blunt question is: What are the institutional church, the hierarchy, and the magisterium waiting for? Why aren't they transforming doctrines, teachings, and practices to remove restrictions on the full participation of women in the church? How can they declare definitively that women cannot be ordained, and insist the subject not be further discussed?

It is worth noting the pointed observation in the *National Catholic Report-*

er (September 15, 2016) by the Rev. Thomas Reese, SJ:

> As a result, religious freedom in its true meaning empowers women to decide for themselves what they will believe and empowers them to challenge the teachings of their own religion if they don't like the way it treats women. Any restrictions on the right of women to challenge religious beliefs and practices is a violation of their religious freedom.

The institutional church should instead be leading the transformation of the People of God to a spirituality that embraces women and men as equals. The secular world, undeniably, is advancing toward a world where women and men are equal partners. We desperately need a spirituality flowing from our church that leaves no doubt that the Church of Jesus Christ is a loving communion where women and men are welcomed equally and without exception.

That's Christian faith. That's Christian spirituality for today's world.

CHAPTER 11

There Is Not One "Reality" Today— That's Not "Relativism" It's "Diversity"

• • • • • •

We take a handful of sand from the endless landscape of awareness around us and call that handful of sand the world.

ROBERT M. PIRSIG
ZEN AND THE ART OF MOTORCYCLE MAINTENANCE

• • • • • •

What we ultimately accept as real drives our belief systems, directs our actions, guides our relationships with others, and informs the way we live our lives. If the God of Judaism, Christianity, and Islam is real to us (even though we all view aspects of that reality differently than our fellow "people of the Book"), then we make decisions and live our lives under that supernatural or a theocentric reality. But the corollary to that obvious truth is that if God is not real to others, in a practical and functional way, they will sometimes make decisions different from our own, though those decisions may be no less well thought out or spiritually-driven than our own.

Our physical bodies, families, friends, culture, society, education (or lack thereof), and personal lived experiences (which differ widely), all contribute to our understanding of what is real in our lives. Essentially, our "reality" is our "spirituality"; yet doesn't our spirituality also determine what we accept as reality? Human history is replete with cultures, civilizations, nations, and especially religions that are convinced that their perception of reality is "the" reality—end of discussion. Yet, many in today's global society find that such a restrained understanding of reality, and such pat answers to complex questions, do not correspond to the tumultuous world that confronts us. Modern experience reveals that there are no easy, all-inclusive answers to the mysteries of life. And what answers we may find don't come exclusively from any one religion.

This chapter's opening epigraph from Robert Pirsig, who died just as this book went to press, comes from his highly acclaimed 1974 novel, *Zen and the Art of Motorcycle Maintenance: An Inquiry Into Values*. At the time of its publication this book introduced an *avant garde* philosophy challenging cherished Aristotelean philosophical views, the black-and-white of Western thought, the fallacious separation of things into the "this" and the disconnected "other." Such dualistic thinking, Pirsig contended, was a wrong turn in European philosophy that denied the need to embrace paradox—not deny or obfuscate it—if we are to live in harmony with a world full of inherent contradiction. The Eastern-oriented approach to reality that Pirsig provoked in his readers—perhaps by now upwards of seven or eight million people—offers an understanding quite different from classical rationalism: that is, the necessary acceptance of rigid and well-defined propositions validated by high authority.

Pirsig's insights, as unorthodox as they seemed in 1974 (his book was rejected for publication 151 times!), are now widely accepted. Pirsig is viewed by some as a prophet, however secular, of our time. He cautions us very simply that how people perceive reality is determined by how open—or closed—we are to accepting the incommensurable and often perplexing diversity of the world around us. Rather than accepting without question a single legitimizing authority and validating pat and packaged answers to questions of immeasurable complexity, a growing number of people, even a growing number of us Catholics, have come to accept uncertainty, doubt, and mystery in our own spiritual journey.

Another contemporary writer, Czech-born French author Milan Kundera, illuminates this idea in his 1984 novel *The Unbearable Lightness of Being*. He describes a complex painting as "On the surface, an intelligible lie; underneath, the unintelligible truth." Pirsig's writing helped awaken in people around the world an appetite for that unintelligible truth.

If we Christians have wide open eyes, not eyes clasped shut against the light, we have a better chance to see a God of and for all. We can understand a universe of God's creation in a way that leads to dialogue with those who do not believe everything we do and, in fact, offers us new eyes to see reality in new ways. As Pirsig admonishes us, we should not "take a handful of sand from the endless landscape of awareness around us and call that handful of sand the world." He expansively observes: "For every fact there is an infinity of hypotheses." And don't we Christians all believe in an infinite God, with infinite love for each and every person, no matter what our orthodoxy?

In recent times we have witnessed a burgeoning of openness to accepting diversity in society that fosters a similar openness to new understandings of reality, unconfined by rigidly orthodox predispositions about what is true. Stephen Hawking, one of the true geniuses of our times, invited an end to certainty when he wrote:

> *A few years ago, the city council of Monza, Italy, barred pet owners from keeping goldfish in curved bowls... saying that it is cruel to keep a fish in a bowl with curved sides because, gazing out, the fish would have a distorted view of reality. But how do we know we have the true, undistorted picture of reality?*

With these observations as a background, I introduce a sixth key ingredient of a spirituality for today that is based on the world's indisputable diversity: Any institution hoping to promulgate a relevant Christian spiritually must reflect, and willingly nurture, diversity in its organizational structures, its doctrines, and its practices. Thus, we Catholics must revisit our understanding of reality in the "Roman" Church. Today's Catholics are truly diverse. We come from an astounding variety of cultures but can be instantaneously connected through technology with views quite different from our own. Can we any longer really say that differences in our lived experiences make one Christian's understanding of the nature of the Divine superior to another's? Even as long ago as 1965, Pope Paul VI, in *Nostra Aestate*, promoted unity and love among people of all nations and creeds. The pope said of even non-Christian religions, "One also is their final goal, God." The Catholic Church of the twenty-first century can no longer look out to the world from curved-sided fish bowls offering only a "distorted view of reality." Catholic spirituality must be transformed by an embrace of diversity itself. Pretty exhortations about the gifts that diversity brings are no longer sufficient. We must embrace and joyfully proclaim its value. We must get out of our fish bowls and swim in the wide ocean abounding with God's myriad people—believers of all faiths and even people of good will who proclaim no faith in God whatsoever.

• • • • • •

We must get out of our fish bowls and swim in the wide ocean abounding with God's myriad people.

• • • • • •

Let us remind ourselves not to confuse our legitimate hope that we Christians "may be one" with the fallacy that we must all be alike. Yet the institutional church continues to push practices and promulgate doctrines that restrict the way we the faithful are allowed to discern the reality of God's unconditional love to closed-ended, westernized, doctrinarian ways. We may hear occasional sermons to the contrary, but how much more often do we hear from the hierarchy that our church is "not a democracy"? Hell, every Catholic knows that. But we just as surely know that the lived experience of the faithful is one of the two sources of Divine revelation (which is much better than democracy anyway)!

It is truly unfortunate in today's world when those in authority in the church consider "collegiality" more as if it were "identity." We have a monolithic hierarchy (albeit headed by a great pope) who were westernized (no matter their country of origin) by their seminary education; who are all men; who are almost all unmarried; who have life tenure in their ordination as bishop; who are promised obedience by their priests. So how is that "collegiality" in communion with the "diversity" of the People of God? Answer: It is not. Our bishops and priests and deacons need to take a hard look at what they consider to be collegiality. We have a right to ask them, in echo of Hawking's query: How do you know you have the true, undistorted picture of reality if you are not even listening to the diversity of the lived experience of all people outside the high walls of your clericalist enclave?

Many faithful Catholics today find the institutional church myopic—an ideological "cultural warrior" instead of the proclaimer of a universal spirituality that is welcoming and inclusive to all, not just those shrouded in orthodoxy. Our criticism is based on what we have already described: their preoccupation with liturgical norms and rubrics; unquestioning adherence to orthodoxy; fears that "relativism" endangers dogma; mistrust of personal intimacy and sexuality.

We Catholics' appreciation for diversity in today's spirituality must not be restricted to just that diversity we find around our own block, within our particular society, but also the diversity that exists in distant cultures and different religions around the world. We all can now call down daily, on a device we hold in the palm of our hand, an endless array of different ideas, cultures, art forms, musical expression (often itself an already cross-cultural pastiche—NPR recently presented a story on Afro-Latin Hip-Hop Jazz Fusion!), religious creeds, and ways of understanding the world.

The institutional church can only provide some much needed leadership in transforming traditional spirituality if it will make itself more open to people of good will in the church, outside the church, in different cultures, of different faiths, and with different life styles. Such openness to others would not be falling into what is so avidly feared by the powers that be in the church as the trap of "relativism." Given today's world and its people, it just no longer makes sense to argue that only *our* "handful of sand" gives us a total view of reality. We no longer live in a world in which imposed views of reality resonate with the lived—and ever more diverse—experience of people today. How much better could this have been presented than in Pope Francis' interview with the Italian newspaper *La Repubblica* (October 1, 2013) when he said:

> *I believe in God, not in a Catholic God. There is no Catholic God, there is God, and I believe in Jesus Christ, his incarnation.*

It is in this same spirit that the renowned Protestant theologian and scholar, Paul Tillich, said: "Sometimes I think it is my mission to bring faith to the faithless and doubt to the faithful." To be successful in developing a Christian spirituality for today's world we need to bring a good dose of doubt to the hierarchy. We must help them help us to question past beliefs so we might all the more clearly see God's continuing revelation to and in all people.

We Catholics are all now witnesses to a continuing explosion of knowledge that does not seek to supersede our spirituality but can illuminate, perhaps even ignite, it. We are compelled by our changing world to see it differently than we once did. How much more powerfully might this eruption of new knowledge detonate our experience of the power of God's love for us and for the world? As John 3:17 quotes Jesus in his dialogue with Nicodemus: "God didn't go to all the trouble of sending his Son merely to point an accusing finger, telling the world how bad it was. He came to help, to put the world right again" (*The Message*). What a dynamic explosion of new knowledge, insights, and human tribal wisdom now enfolds us. Different people, different ideas, different cultures, different ways to love our neighbor as ourselves. We Christians should not fear and shy from the diversity before us. We should instead gather it into baskets as if it were manna fallen from heaven.

Today's spiritual reality is at its core an awakening to diversity that in turn awakens us to the grace that is all around us. The Holy Spirit calls us continuously to transform ourselves as we read the *signs of the times*. It is in the shining light of modern reality that we are truly free to communally discern what the Holy Spirit is revealing to us, the People of God, today. The Holy Spirit speaks to us today in so many tongues, not just in a voice a nomadic shepherd may have understood, but sometimes that of the holder of an M.A. in Psychology, an advanced degree in astrophysics, or a Ph.D. in comparative religions. (Wow! The Holy Spirit better watch out for accusations of being a relativist.)

In times of great innovation such as ours, events and ideas do not always blossom in linear ways but often amid disorder and confusion. That means, just as Pope Francis has said many times, things will sometimes be somewhat messy in the church. And, that's very much okay with many faithful Catholics—myself included!

The institutional church today is quick to judge who is right, who is wrong, who may or may not receive the body and the blood of Jesus Christ, for example, or who lives a life that they can label "disordered," or who may decide what is religious truth and chastise those it labels "heretics." We live in a world today that is quantitatively and qualitatively vastly different from the world "The Church" (writ-large) knew millennia, or centuries, or even just decades, ago. Yet, most Catholics know that certain dogmas must be re-interpreted in the light of new and advanced knowledge, of a more complete understanding of our world, rather than setting in stone forever anything and everything we once believed.

Anthony de Mello, SJ, an Indian priest, psychotherapist, spiritual writer, and storyteller, illustrates this point in his book *The Song of the Bird*. He tells a story about the devil and a friend taking a walk together. A man ahead of them stops suddenly and picks something up from the ground. At that point the friend asks the devil:

> *"What did that man find?"*
> *The devil responds, "A piece of truth."*
> *The friend says to the devil, "Doesn't that disturb you?*
> *"No," says the devil, "I shall let him make a belief out of it."*

For de Mello, "A religious belief is a signpost pointing the way to truth. People who cling tenaciously to the signpost are prevented from moving towards the truth because they have the false feeling that they already possess it."

Past perceptions of reality enforced a segregation between people with geographical and/or doctrinal borders. But modern reality ultimately allows few physical borders to separate people, much less doctrinal ones. Today the reality is that people, even those with a shared culture, even those who embrace in faith their Catholic religion, do not accept the validity of each and every proclamation of the magisterium, or find such orthodoxy pertinent to the struggles of their daily lives. That does not make us bad Catholics. That very diversity is a singular and defining expression of Jesus' inclusive message.

This approach was startlingly advanced by Bishop Robert Lynch in a message to his Diocese of St. Petersburg on October 28, 2016:

> *So there is little to be gained and lots to be lost by continuing to fight cultural battles in an evolving culture with worn out logic and words that today's younger Catholic membership does not wish to hear or rejects outright. We will be far more attractive to the future generations by not pursuing a pastoral approach that is angry at those who do not "buy the whole package" but still wish to belong to a community which evinces Christ's compassion and understanding of the moment. Will we still teach sin and forgiveness? You betcha! But if you are a believer in the inspiration which is Pope Francis, then you do so always with his openness to those who may not get it, in sum or parts, but who also wish to make Christ present in the world. Be glad there is some fruit on the tree still!*

We need to develop a Christian spirituality that is meaningful for the third millennium. It should be based on Anthony de Mello's advice: "Spirituality means waking up." We must all wake up to the reality that we need a spirituality steeped in the rich diversity of today's world:

- that is expansive enough to serve people where they are on their life journeys, not where we wish them to be;
- that is adaptable enough to fit into the reality of different cultures, not a (Western) monolithic culture controlled by a few;
- that is wise enough to be aware that people are self-actualizing, no longer obedient for obedience's sake;
- that is comfortable with the idea that people (especially young people) today see the beauty of Christianity in its innovation and creativity, not its conformity, rote rituals, and doctrinal compliance.

We will at last unveil a truly catholic (small c) spirituality that is bold and imaginative, reflecting the righteous and prophetic sense of the continuous revelation of God's unconditional love.

That's Christian faith. That's Christian spirituality for today's world.

CHAPTER 12

Freedom of Religion/Conscience— A Doubled-edged Sword

• • • • • •

I shall drink to the Pope, if you please;
still, to conscience first, and to the Pope afterwards.

BLESSED CARDINAL JOHN HENRY NEWMAN

• • • • • •

The Catholic Church—its hierarchy, theologians, canon lawyers, ordained and vowed religious, liturgists, educators, and all the faithful who will contribute to a "catholic" spirituality for the twenty-first century—must reflect seriously on the individual's essential freedom to respond in a personal way to the Gospel within the framework of our existing church culture. The institutional church seems either unaware of, or in denial of, the fact that freedom of religion among the emerging Catholic faithful includes freedom *within* religion.

That two-edged sword must no longer be ignored. The institutional church since Vatican II has certainly acted as a culture warrior across the political landscape, holding high the banner of freedom of religion. However, when it comes to its tolerance of freedom for its own faithful who dare to challenge some of its positions, we hear a different story. Heralding freedom but in fact denying freedom of its faithful to disagree with the magisterium does not reflect Jesus' pastoral approach to spirituality and makes no sense for today's society. Many now are openly saying: "Don't talk to me about freedom of religion if I don't have freedom within my Catholic religion to question and challenge *our*, not just *your*, church."

How do we Catholic faithful with different views from the hierarchy—sometimes including the pope—assess and defend our level of freedom within our church today? Have any of the actions of the hierarchy demonstrated that we have freedom to openly question or express our religious doubts or disagreements? The answer is yes, and it is yes because of the church's longstanding position summarized so pithily by an Anglican turned Roman Catholic Cardinal, Blessed John Henry Newman: "We can believe what we choose. We are answerable for what we choose to believe."

The Catholic tradition on freedom of religion is a double-edged sword. One edge of the sword repulses any outside force that would interfere with the church's right to proclaim what it believes is right. But the opposite sharp edge hews down any of us with the temerity to challenge cherished institutional positions. But even the church can't have it both ways in today's world.

Freedom of religion/conscience is the seventh and final ingredient necessary for a meaningful spirituality for today's Christian. We faithful today must be allowed to freely share our personal spiritual insights among the People of God; to seek insights from other religions and cultures; and to express our questions and challenges without institutional recrimination. This does not mean that the institutional church must surrender its teaching authority as it engages with its members and the world; but neither should the faithful be driven from the church for wanting to engage in open and candid dialogue with their fellow church members. Because the faithful now see the world differently, church leaders must also learn to see things differently. They must be open to listening to the lived experience of the faithful and not fear that every question or challenge threatens them.

To attain such openness will be very difficult for the Catholic Church. It has promulgated—and for centuries thrived upon—a culture of strict authority. In our distant past, most of the faithful docilely accepted a top-down power structure. But those times when the majority of worshippers automatically complied with authority are long past. Just as we Catholics have been liberated socially, politically, sexually, and economically, it is high time for us to find liberation in our spirituality as well. The institutional church needs to help us—not hinder us—in finding that freedom. The key, in my opinion, is a return to the Catholic teaching that freedom of religion also demands freedom of conscience.

Even though those in the leadership of the church acknowledge that they are witnessing an historic paradigm shift on this issue, many still consider themselves somehow immune from the sea of changes in modern society. Staunch traditionalists in the hierarchy cling to the belief that they alone are the protectors of the "deposit of faith." They hold that their ordination infuses them with the particular power to protect dogma and morality, divinely transmitted through them, for the church and all its people for all time. Thus, their mantra, continued *ad nauseum*: The church is not a democracy.

No it is not. The church is a "monarchy" in which conscience is both king and queen! It is not only possible but probable and desirable that we will have many "good" Catholics in the future who disagree with today's church teachings on women's ordination, gay marriage, even beginning- and end-of-life issues. That should not be feared, it should be celebrated, because it will show that Catholics understand, believe in, and act upon the freedom of religion/conscience.

What the hierarchy seem not to have considered is the way the global transition to a freer society, the ongoing empowerment of the individual, has expressed itself as a demand for greater freedom of religious thought as well. The idea of true freedom of religion invites competition. Creeds are not so much to be received as to be considered and chosen. Competition—whether in markets, ideas, or religions—is the mechanism by which freedom illuminates and finally transforms reality. But competition within the institutional church is quashed by the very nature of its vertical structure. The only sanctioned competition today, usually hidden, is the jockeying for position of players who are all tainted by clericalism. Paul, with typical clarity, saw this coming in his first letter to his protégé Timothy:

> *The whole point of what we're urging is simply love—love uncontaminated by self-interest and counterfeit faith, a life open to God. Those who fail to keep to this point soon wander off into cul-de-sacs of gossip. They set themselves up as experts on religious issues, but haven't the remotest idea of what they're holding forth with such imposing eloquence.*

1 Timothy 1:5-7, *The Message*

If these concerns about clericalism seem overblown, consider the congruent opinion of a current, undisputed church insider, Pope Francis. In April 2016 he wrote to Cardinal Marc Ouellet of Quebec, Canada, about how the institutional church might better serve the faithful People of God:

> *It is good for us to remember that the Church is not an elite of priests, of consecrated people, of bishops—but that everyone forms the Holy Faithful People of God...*
>
> *Clericalism, far from giving impulse to diverse contributions and proposals, turns off, little by little, the prophetic fire from which the entire Church is called to give testimony in the heart of its peoples...*
>
> *Clericalism forgets that the visibility and the sacramentality of the Church belongs to all the people of God and not only an elect or illuminated few.*
>
> *It is illogical, and even impossible, to think that we as pastors should have the monopoly on solutions for the many challenges that modern life presents to us. On the contrary, we must remain at the side of our people, accompanying them in their work and stimulating that capable imagination of responding to current problems.*

A new and transformed spirituality in the church must reveal unequivocally at its very core this trust in the faithful to seek the good and the truth of Jesus and his Gospel. That will be the consummated reality of a spirituality sparked by "freedom within religion" in the church. A spirituality for today's world must no longer be compelled at the edge of the sword of authority. Spirituality must be built upon a framework that the Holy Spirit's grace inspires in the hearts, minds, faith, actions, and questions of the People of God.

• • • • • •

Spirituality must be built upon a framework that the Holy Spirit's grace inspires in the hearts, minds, faith, actions, and questions of the People of God.

• • • • • •

In today's globalized society people have at their fingertips the ability to witness and even participate in a whole range of human societies, cultures, and religions. As never before in history, people are intimately aware of the myriad and beautiful ways other people experience God. Symbols, rituals, and perceptions vastly different from traditional Christian viewpoints can help the People of God realize new ways to practice a spirituality unfettered by the past. The institutional church must not discourage and hide from this expanded awareness. It should rather encourage this freedom as a wonderful opportunity to embrace new insights into a Christian spirituality that frees the People of God to encounter the never-ending revelation of God's mystery on earth.

This freedom of religion/conscience that we Catholics have by virtue of our baptism is well described by Father Peter Phan, a theologian born in Vietnam and the past president of the Catholic Theological Society of America. Phan's writings and teachings have drawn close scrutiny from a variety of church authorities, but his words have resonated with the rest of us. In his book, *Religious Identity and Belonging Amidst Diversity and Pluralism: Challenges and Opportunities for Church and Theology,* Phan states:

> *Religious pluralism then is not just a matter of fact but also a matter of principle. That is, non-Christian religions may be seen as part of the plan*

of Divine Providence and endowed with a particular role in this history of salvation.

Many church leaders are unready to accept this freedom, this "competition" for better understandings. They decline to acknowledge, however, that many faithful Catholics today gain spiritual insight from sources outside the church that resonate more closely with our lived experience. The institutional church engages in a losing battle when it tries to prevent the exploration of a relevant and open Christian spirituality by the faithful today, a spirituality that recognizes that we have to listen to our conscience both before and after we consult church teaching.

I have enough enduring Catholic faith to enter religion's competitive free market with a light heart. I believe that the great good news of Jesus Christ, set free, will be attractive enough in the global free market to people struggling, as I am, to embrace the astounding love and mystery of God. I see all around me a growing number of people in the Church who also have enough Catholic faith to proclaim Jesus Christ's unconditional love for all on this globe, even as they discern ever more deeply what and how they believe. So why don't some church leaders have enough Catholic faith to enter that free market of ideas and beliefs and become "all things to all people," as I titled a previous book? The Catholic faith's creed of limitless love radiating from the Trinitarian God is so compelling and marketable that the Holy Spirit may have been the first successful "free market capitalist" in the world!

In case my free-market analogy regarding a topic of such profound gravity seems flippant, let me consult a more conventional expression of the critically important idea I am trying to convey. Consider the words of Archbishop Oswald Gracias of Mumbai, India, in a 2006 interview with the *National Catholic Reporter* when he said:

The Holy Spirit guides us in a particular direction at a particular time, and today we're being led towards enculturation.... In Asian societies, religion is seen as a necessary part of the culture. I believe the West has got to learn to respond to the signs of the times. Change and adaptation is necessary, and maybe the churches of the South, especially in Asia, can offer an example. Today, we try to be open to the Spirit with self-confidence, believing that enculturation is not going to take the church to the ruins.

Such an approach to enliven and transform our spirituality in the Church today would not make us any less Christian. In fact, I believe a new-found freedom in the church to embrace our own freedom of religion/conscience will make us even better Catholics. An important roadblock, of course, is the not unnatural fear that we faithful, given the opportunity for freedom within our religion, may become confused and begin to doubt church orthodoxy. Yes, this certainly will lead some of us to challenge and doubt the church. But, let's have some faith in the wisdom of people! Let's not forget that the Holy Spirit is in the hearts and minds of all the faithful, not just the hierarchy.

Pope Francis himself anticipated such fears. At his morning Mass homily on December 14, 2016, he said poignantly:

The great ones can afford to doubt and this is wonderful. They are confident in their vocation, but every time the Lord shows them a new road along the journey they begin to doubt. But this isn't orthodox, this is heretical; this isn't the Messiah I was expecting."

Indeed, the Christian God is full of surprises. Today's spirituality must be freely open to the vast new cultural knowledge and religious insights we encounter as we go about our daily lives lifting that shroud from *The Veiled Christ.*

Let us open our eyes, our minds, our imaginations, and our hearts, on our own journey to Emmaus, to the Messiah we were not expecting.

Surprise! That's Christian faith. That's Christian spirituality for today's world.

CONCLUSION

Building a World in Which God Would Be Happy to Live

· · · · · ·

God is in need of each of us if holiness is to be achieved in the world. Our actions have cosmic impact. The very presence of God in the world is dependent upon what you and I do.

DAVID ELLENSON

· · · · · ·

In his book *Jews and Judaism in the 21st Century*, Rabbi David Ellenson, a former President of Hebrew Union College-Jewish Institute of Religion, a distinguished scholar, and leader of the Jewish Reform Movement, writes an essay titled, *Building a World in Which God Would Be Happy to Live*. Isn't that an excellent paraphrase of the words with which Jesus taught us to pray, "...thy kingdom come... on earth as it is in heaven"?

I have attempted in this book to point out that Christian spirituality is nothing less than the totality of who we are, what we believe, and what we actually do as faithful followers of Jesus Christ. Christian spirituality must not be confused with formulaic prayers, rituals, creeds, dogmas, or doctrines. For us Christians, spirituality should begin and end with the God introduced to us by and through Jesus, whom we recognize as the ultimate arbiter of his "Abba's" true nature. That reality continues to unfold and reveal to us each day new insights into the mysteries of creation. Our spirituality is a gift that not only brings each of us to the church as a community of believers, but also brings Jesus' message of universal love and forgiveness to all people, regardless of where they may be on their own journey to meaningfulness.

Rabbi Ellenson's straightforward observation about our responsibility to bring holiness into the world speaks to me of what Christian spirituality is all about. Once and for all, we must understand that God is not present to the world because of clerical dictums, historic professions of creed, or even the existence of an institutional church that is millennia old; rather, according to the rabbi, "The very presence of God in the world is dependent upon what you and I do." That just might be one of the many good reasons why we Christians, along with our Jewish and Muslim brethren, believe women and men were created in God's image and likeness.

As we conclude our brief exploration of a contemporary Christian spirituality, each of us must answer for ourselves whether the church needs—or does not need—a transformed spirituality for today's world.

To answer that question honestly, which I believe we are called to do, each of us alone and all of us together, it will help to recall the beautiful image of Giuseppe Sanmartino's magnificent marble sculpture, *The Veiled Christ*. Recall the unbelievable genius of the marble veil draped upon the lifeless body of Jesus in the tomb just before he became the resurrected Christ. Though the veil shrouded the body of Jesus, there was no doubt that it was truly the lifeless Jesus there in that tomb. Yet then he rose from beneath that shroud, the Christ, the Anointed One.

I ask you to imagine a group of parishioners sitting in the pews of any Catholic Mass. (Mind you, many who have already left the church will be missing.) Now, we may be easily lulled into the perception that we see those sitting there clearly. But look again. There is still a veil cloaking the innermost thoughts and deepest impulses of faith of each person awaiting the celebration of the Eucharist. Yes, they are the faithful, but let's imagine we can slowly lift that thin veil lying so peacefully over all those in the pews. As we lift that veil that obscures the faithful, can we not see a number who:

- use artificial birth control?
- are civilly married or divorced and did not get an annulment?
- live together as husband and wife without a sacramental marriage?
- are having pre-marital sex?
- are gay, lesbian, transsexual, transgender?
- do not give "definitive assent" to the argument that women cannot be ordained priests?
- are not in lockstep with every pronouncement of church doctrine?
- believe that the clericalized leadership of the Church is in need of radical transformation?

I am afraid to lift that veil any further. I do not understand how anyone, especially so many of our bishops, can continue to refuse to face reality and see what is right in front of us.

Here is what Bishop Robert Lynch, Diocese of St. Petersburg, said on October 28, 2016 about the notion of "winnowing down" the church to those who agree with the entire magisterium without reservation or disagreement. He said:

> At one point I mentioned that an American bishop had delivered a talk within the last two days in which he publicly embraced a position that it might be good for the Church to clear its membership rolls of many people and perhaps start to rebuild the church from a smaller core of a more orthodox, committed few. I told the men that this was a largely unspoken and unpublished concept that had silently and secretly emerged in the late eighties and nineties, emanating from some US bishops serving in Rome. Now it seemed to me that the strategy was finally publicly articulated. I also told them that I was appalled then when I first heard of it decades ago and am even more so now because it would seem to me to be a rejection of the pastoral vision of Pope Francis which I find so challenging and exciting.

The provocative title of this book, *Do You Know What You Are Doing, God?* is not flippant, or irreverent, or a mistake. It's the very question we should be asking ourselves if we are truly seeking a deeper and more meaningful spirituality for today's world. Such profound questions illuminate our faith and light our way as we draw nearer and nearer to a true Christian spirituality. The acceptance of this conundrum, that we must doubt to believe, helps us understand that our faith's strength and validity is in direct proportion to our willingness to question and search for insight into the great, grand mysteries of God, life, and creation. That very inquisitiveness transforms our faith seeking understanding into an enduring spirituality instead of a rigid, unquestioned, inherited ideology. The more we question our beliefs, the greater do we find ourselves in awe of God's creation and in God's unconditional love for us.

The natural corollary to my premise is that Christian spirituality not only fails to grow but weakens as we stop questioning our beliefs. Without questions and doubts we confuse spirituality with ideology. The less we question our faith, the more we delude ourselves into thinking we possess a fixed knowledge of the unknowable. We even fool ourselves into thinking we can control the how, what, where, why, and when of other people's personal relationship to God. It just doesn't work that way. Admit at least that!

I believe we will have a better insight into our faith and into the rich depths that our spirituality can reach because the question, "Do you know what you are doing, God?" will inevitably give us the courage to realize we must first ask:

- Pope, cardinals and bishops. Do you really know what you are doing?
- Priests and religious. Do you really know what you are doing?
- Conservatives and progressives. Do you really know what you are doing?
- Religions, nations, and all people on the globe. Do you really know what you are doing?

- Finally, of course, look into a mirror. Do I really know what I am doing?

A Christian spirituality that encourages people to thoughtfully question the institutional church and their own, perhaps calcified, thinking will offer a pathway to finding God's kingdom on earth as it is in heaven. It is this very insight that Pope Francis shared with those assembled at his November 23, 2016 weekly general audience:

We do not need to be afraid of questions and doubts because they are the beginning of a path of knowledge and going deeper; one who does not ask questions cannot progress either in knowledge or in faith.

No way can a Christian spirituality for today's world in any way support exclusion of others, failure to think for one's self, or blind obedience. Even Saint Augustine, as far back as the fourth century, tells us, "Believers are also thinkers; in believing they think, and in thinking they also believe.... If faith does not think, it is nothing." Jesus' church will be made real and holy in today's world because of a spirituality that gathers all of us sinners and all people who freely, that is, of their own choice, follow him.

Let us remember Pelagius' beautiful description of the core goodness that is found in creation. We see that goodness only because of "the shafts of divine light" that penetrate that thin veil dividing heaven and earth. As much as we try, in our prayers, our deliberations, or ecclesiastical convocations—even in this book!—we will never totally remove that veil shrouding divine mystery, never penetrate that great cloud of unknowing. However, I pray that together, as the entire People of God, our quest for an ever-deeper understanding of how God works in our lives may help ignite an ever-brighter spirituality for today's world. Then one day we may surprise even ourselves when we are finally able to cry out, "Wow, God! You really do know what you are doing."

Go ahead and do it. Lift that veil and see that truly Jesus lives in our hearts forever!

That's Christian faith. That's Christian spirituality for today's world.

RELATED TITLES

ALL THINGS TO ALL PEOPLE
A Catholic Church for the Twenty-First Century
Brother Louis DeThomasis, FSC

Buckle up for an old-fashioned but good-spirited Catholic brawl about the future of the Church in the twenty-first century. The author takes on all the hot-button topics in the church today. He offers new insights on clericalism, infallibility, conscience, vocation, and the "sense of the faithful" as a source of divine revelation. And he offers a recipe for transforming the Catholic Church in a way that will allow it to proclaim the message of Jesus Christ to a twenty-first century world that is more globalized and diverse than ever before. (128 pages, paperback)

THE SILENT SCHISM
Healing the Serious Split in the Catholic Church
Brother Louis DeThomasis, FSC, and Sister Cynthia Nienhaus, CSA

Brother Louis De Thomasis and Sr. Cynthia Nienhaus use Pope Francis' "grammar of simplicity" to describe the current schism happening in the Catholic Church worldwide and to offer solutions for how to heal it. They call on both traditionalists and progressives in the church to recapture the mission of Jesus to bring about the reign of God "on earth, as it is in heaven." (128 pages, paperback)

FLYING IN THE FACE OF TRADITION
Listening to the Lived Experience of the Faithful
Brother Louis DeThomasis, FSC

Explores the Catholic notion of "tradition" as a source of revelation as a way out of the current quandary in the Catholic Church. (102 pages, paperback and hardcover)

DYNAMICS OF CATHOLIC EDUCATION
Letting the Catholic School Be School
Brother Louis DeThomasis, FSC

Addresses the important role of Catholic education in spreading the Christian message to new generations in new ways. (144 pages, paperback)

Available from booksellers or call 800-397-2282
www.actapublications.com

Other Books from In Extenso Press

CATHOLIC BOY BLUES: A Poet's Journey of Healing,
by Norbert Krapf, 224 pages, paperback

CATHOLIC WATERSHED: The Chicago Ordination Class of 1969
and How They Helped Change the Church,
by Michael P. Cahill, 394 pages, paperback

CHRISTIAN CONTEMPLATIVE LIVING:
Six Connecting Points, by Thomas M. Santa, CSSR, 126 pages, paperback

GREAT MEN OF THE BIBLE: A Guide for Guys,
by Martin Pable, OFM Cap, 216 pages, paperback

THE GROUND OF LOVE AND TRUTH: Reflections on Thomas
Merton's Relationship with the Woman Known as "M,"
by Suzanne Zuercher, OSB, 120 pages, paperback

HOPE: One Man's Journey of Discovery from Tormented Child to Social Worker
to Spiritual Director, by Marshall Jung, 172 pages, paperback

MASTER OF CEREMONIES: A Novel,
by Donald Cozzens, 288 pages, paperback and hardcover

NAVIGATING ALZHEIMER'S: 12 Truths about Caring for Your Loved One,
by Mary K. Doyle, 112 pages, paperback

PISTACO: A Tale of Love in the Andes,
by Lynn F. Monahan, 298 pages, paperback and hardcover-

SHRINKING THE MONSTER: Healing the Wounds of Our Abuse,
by Norbert Krapf, 234 pages, paperback

THE UNPUBLISHED POET: On Not Giving Up on Your Dream,
by Marjorie L. Skelly, 160 pages, paperback

WAYWARD TRACKS: Revelations about fatherhood, faith, fighting with your spouse,
surviving Girl Scout camp…, by Mark Collins, 104 pages, paperback

WE THE (LITTLE) PEOPLE, artwork by ISz, 50 plates, paperback

YOUR SECOND TO LAST CHAPTER: Creating a Meaningful Life on Your Own
Terms, by Paul Wilkes, 120 pages, paperback and hardcover

BAPTIZED FOR THIS MOMENT: Rediscovering Grace All Around Us,
by Stephen Paul Bouman, 168 pages, paperback

AVAILABLE FROM BOOKSELLERS
OR FROM 800-397-2282 • INEXTENSOPRESS.COM
DISTRIBUTED EXCLUSIVELY BY ACTA PUBLICATIONS